SIMPLY MEDITERRANEAN COOKING

SIMPLY MEDITERRANEAN COOKING

Robert ROSE

SIMPLY MEDITERRANEAN COOKING

Copyright © 1998 Byron Ayanoglu

For complete cataloguing data, see page 6.

DESIGN AND PAGE COMPOSITION:	MATTHEWS COMMUNICATIONS DESIGN
PHOTOGRAPHY:	MARK T. SHAPIRO
ART DIRECTION/FOOD PHOTOGRAPHY:	SHARON MATTHEWS
FOOD STYLIST:	KATE BUSH
PROP STYLIST:	MIRIAM GEE
MANAGING EDITOR:	PETER MATTHEWS
INDEXER:	BARBARA SCHON
COLOR SCANS & FILM:	POINTONE GRAPHICS

Cover photo: TAGINE CHICKEN WITH LEMON, OLIVES AND GRAPES *(PAGE 104)*

Distributed in the U.S. by:
Firefly Books (U.S.) Inc.
P.O. Box 1338
Ellicott Station
Buffalo, NY   14205

Distributed in Canada by:
Stoddart Publishing Co. Ltd.
34 Lesmill Road
North York, Ontario
M3B 2T6

ORDER LINES
Tel: (416) 499-8412
Fax: (416) 499-8313

ORDER LINES
Tel: (416) 445-3333
Fax: (416) 445-5967

Published by: Robert Rose Inc. • 156 Duncan Mill Road, Suite 12
Toronto, Ontario, Canada M3B 2N2   Tel: (416) 449-3535

Printed in Canada

1234567 BP 01 00 99 98

CONTENTS

THE NEW MEDITERRANEAN   11

THE MEDITERRANEAN KITCHEN   13

APPETIZERS   21

SALADS   49

FISH AND SEAFOOD   69

CHICKEN   95

MEAT   111

PASTA AND GRAINS   147

DESSERTS   171

INDEX   183

Canadian Cataloguing in Publication Data

Ayanoglu, Byron
    Simply Mediterranean cooking

Includes index.
ISBN 1-896503-68-3

1. Cookery, Mediterranean. I. Title.

TX725.M43A92 1998   641.59'1822   C97-932611-7

THESE RECIPES

ARE DEDICATED

TO THE LEGACY OF

OUR MOTHERS,

DESPINA AYANOGLU

AND

FREDA KEMEZYS

ACKNOWLEDGEMENTS

MANY THANKS TO

Bob Dees • Sharon and Peter Matthews • Martha Reilly
P. A. Super Marché (5029 ave. du Parc, Montreal)

and also to

Jonah, Chas and Ralph Benmergui • Jack Blum • Sharon Corder • Charlotte Dix •
Barbara Fitchette • Androula Haalboom • Daniaile Jarry • Jon Kalina •
Nathalie Kalina • Soula Mbozi • Marion, Amnon and Josh Medad •
Anastasia Jarry-Mihalka • George Mihalka • Asher, Suzanne and Paulette Motola •
Leslie Orr • Tom Rack • Juan Rodriguez • Aziza Saleb • Leo Schipani •
Jane, Kate, Michael and Jaimie Sutherland • Cristallia Vassilyadou • Harry X

and to all the other people who have helped to make this book possible.

PHOTO PROP CREDITS

The publisher and authors wish to express their appreciation to the following suppliers
of props used in the food photography appearing in this book:

BOHEMEX, TORONTO
•
HOMEFRONT, TORONTO

WELCOME TO THE WORLD OF
OLIVE-OIL COOKERY; IT'LL MAKE
YOU HAPPY. AS THOMAS
JEFFERSON ONCE WROTE:
"THE OLIVE TREE IS SURELY THE
RICHEST TREE OF HEAVEN."

THE NEW MEDITERRANEAN

Mediterranean food has been all the rage for some three or four thousand years. The warm azure sea and the sun-drenched, olive-groved, magnolia-scented shores that surround it — the "cradle of Western civilization" — is the home of the world's greatest collective cuisine.

With its perfect climate and four distinct seasons, the Mediterranean is a meeting point for cultures of the East, West, North and South. Its various native cuisines have been visited (and invaded) by culinary notions and inspirations from all continents, melding into the particular cooking styles that we know as Italian, Greek, French, Spanish, North African and Middle Eastern. This is an amalgam of olive oil and garlic and herbs, with noodles and rice, seafood and lamb, and the most fragrant, toothsome fruits and vegetables on the planet.

In this book, my partner Algis Kemezys and I have attempted to transport the essence of Mediterranean cooking to kitchens in North America. Here you'll find recipes that are simplified for easy execution, adapted to suit the availability of ingredients on this side of the Atlantic, and modified (modernized, if you will) to reflect contemporary tastes for lower-fat, full-flavor, international palate teasers.

These are recipes that speak the language of sunshine tastes and textures, of lightness and fun. They celebrate recreational eating that is nourishing and digestible, as it brings smiles of contentment. There are recipes for everyday family meals, as well as festive occasions. And there are recipes with which to stay cool and active in summer, and warm and happy in winter.

The cuisine explored in this book was no random choice. Neither did my love for and deep understanding of Mediterranean cooking suddenly come upon me while on a package tour to Italy and Greece. This is the food with which I've lived forever — during my first 12 years as a member of the Greek community of Istanbul, and then the rest of my life as part of the Greek diaspora in Canada, England, the U.S., Mexico and India.

The essence of Mediterranean cuisine, of course, is olive oil — the only foodstuff that I almost always crave and cannot seem to do without. (In

India I tracked it down in pharmacies, where they sell it as a skin tonic.) Olive oil is the constant thread that unites all the cuisines of the Mediterranean nations: It works so seamlessly with all of the region's wonderful aromatics, enhances its delicate meats and fishes, and gives meaning to its various culinary tricks and techniques.

If left up to me, everything in this book would be drenched in olive oil, as it is in the countries of origin. Fortunately, Algis is much more concerned than I am about modern sensibilities, and together we've re-invented these timeless recipes using less oil and more ingenuity.

Try them, they're wonderful.

Byron Ayanoglu
MONTREAL, 1998

THE MEDITERRANEAN KITCHEN

Back in the home countries, the kitchen is an active, round-the-clock workroom. People think nothing of working all day to create a meal. Sadly, much as we in North America like to eat well, there aren't many of us willing to put in such an effort (even if we had the time).

There are shortcuts available to us, of course, such as canned beans and tomatoes, commercially prepared stocks and ready-peeled garlic. Use them if you have to, but never stint on simmering, especially where meats are concerned. It is impossible to achieve the flavor and textures of the various meat "stews" in this book if you try to accelerate the process by cooking them over too-high heat.

There is a saving grace. The stews in question (like all stews) actually improve with an overnight rest in the fridge, followed by a gentle rewarming the next day. So if you're able to plan ahead, prepare them the night before. It entails about 20 minutes of work, and then the inevitable slow simmer while you watch TV. Just make sure the stew cools down completely before refrigerating; otherwise it will sour.

As noted earlier, I have reduced the fat content of these dishes. The most valuable tool for achieving this is the nonstick frying pan. Unheard of in the Mediterranean, it allows us to perform, with just a token amount of olive oil, all the sautéing and the pre-frying upon which many of these recipes depend.

What about the cost of the ingredients? Expense can be a concern, especially when it comes to some types of fish and seafood. So I've suggested minimum quantities, often setting out recipes that will serve two instead of four. As far as I'm concerned, no one should have to shy away from recipes because of cost. Of course, if you're feeling flush, it won't hurt to use an extra 4 oz (125 g) of, say, shrimps. The recipe will work just as well and it'll give you additional bites of a favorite ingredient.

Speaking of seafood — and, by the way, also of fish — I cannot overemphasize the importance of finding a fishmonger you can trust. Too much of our sea-produce, especially in our inland cities, arrives either in a dubious state (if fresh), or is sold defrosted from frozen (as if it were fresh). Only the person behind the counter knows for sure. A good fish-monger will also perform invaluable services like filleting, deboning and selling you fish heads for making fish stock.

And a general word about garlic, herbs and spices. Throughout this book I've recommended the minimum quantities required to achieve a flavor that will appeal to the "average" palate. If extra adventurous, you can always double the quantities of things like cumin, cinnamon, allspice, chilies, all the herbs, and also garlic without in the least jeopardizing the final effect — if anything, you'll enhance it.

Just keep in mind that Mediterranean cooking (and therefore eating) has evolved over millennia, adapting itself endlessly and incorporating ideas from everywhere. It is lusty, joyful food, and it must be entered into in that spirit. It is also fairly foolproof: There is nothing much you can do to ruin it. (Well, you could burn the garlic or the onions at the beginning of the process; so don't.) Cook with a light hand, and your efforts will be rewarded by many a memorable meal.

THE MEDITERRANEAN PANTRY

Ingredients define and dictate cuisine. Trying to recreate a far-away style of cooking on this continent demands a bit of adapting and a bit of making-do. Obviously we can't achieve the exact flavors of things Mediterranean, but we can come close. We are helped along by the millions of Mediterranean natives who live here, and who cultivate, manufacture and import the essential ingredients of their beloved food. Here I offer you a list of pantry and fridge items (in order of importance) that are widely available and are indispensable to the recipes in this book. They'll also be lovely in whatever else you cook.

OLIVE OIL

The fuel of Mediterranean cuisine, this golden fluid hardly needs any further introduction. It has become so popular (partly because of its alleged therapeutic properties, but absolutely because of its wonderful flavor) that the forces of supply and demand have pushed its price skyward. Olive oil comes in many classifications, but there are only two that need concern us: "Virgin" and not.

"Virgin" refers to the method of extracting oil that involves simply pressing the olives themselves (much like a winemaker's "premier cru") — no heat, no tricks; just unadorned olive juice that is meant to be eaten raw, as a condiment on salads, pasta, fish, whatever. A bottle of virgin olive oil (or "extra virgin", which contains only the very first pressing of oil) can run you anywhere from $10 to $60. So unless you're a millionaire, this is obviously not an oil for frying. In this book, any time the taste of fine olive oil is required, I call for the extra virgin variety.

Regular olive oil is extracted from the pulp that is left over after the virgin stuff has been collected, usually with the aid of heat and other processing. While it doesn't offer the nuanced flavor and aroma of extra virgin oil, it's a lot cheaper — and is just fine for sautéing. This type of oil is used in almost every recipe here, and I refer to it simply as "olive oil."

GARLIC

Garlic is garlic. It is wonderful. It works raw for salad dressings (pressed to allow it to spread its flavor), as well as finely chopped and cooked in sauces. It is also fabulous just peeled and used whole in stews; it keeps its shape, but becomes soft and sweet. Apparently it is also good for the health. Its only problem is that it hates being burnt. Then it turns bitter.

LEMON

The entire Mediterranean is taken up by lemon trees, or so it would seem. Lemon juice is served with everything, most probably because its flavor works so well with that of olive oil. Another wonderful source of flavor is lemon zest, which is the yellow part of its peel (the white part is unpleasantly bitter). You can harvest the zest either with a grater (dangerous for the knuckles) or with a "zester" — one of those cute implements that make visiting a specialty kitchen store so much fun. The zester, which looks like a tiny set of brass knuckles, takes the zest off in ribbons; these can be used as is, or finely chopped if the recipe calls for it.

BALSAMIC VINEGAR

All vinegars — white wine, red wine, cider, even plain white — are fine in their proper place, if used in moderation. Balsamic vinegar, a secret of Italian cuisine that became an instant hit when it was "discovered" by modern gourmets some years ago, is an exception. It is sweet and tasty and can actually be consumed (and enjoyed) on its own. It is the dieter's best friend, as it makes an excellent dressing for salads without requiring the addition of any oil to temper its acidity. I use it a lot in cooking, where sourness is important and lemon juice would be too tame.

TOMATOES

Although only a relatively recent arrival in the Mediterranean (about the 16th century), tomatoes have taken over as the ingredient of choice for sauces of all kinds. Obviously, nothing beats a fresh tomato in August, but it's only August for one month in 12. Recognizing this, I've indicated in many recipes where canned tomatoes will serve as an adequate stand-in. A few absolutely must have fresh tomatoes, however. Luckily, these are available — albeit expensive and imperfect — even out of season.

Sun-dried tomatoes, like balsamic vinegar and extra virgin olive oil, are very popular these days, and widely available. They add a spectacular perkiness to many dishes and I use them quite a bit. Just keep in mind that they are quite salty, so ease up on the salt when using them. Also note that when we specify a quantity of "1", we actually mean half of the original tomato. You'll often find the two halves still attached to each other; so treat such a pair as 2 sun-dried tomatoes.

Tomato paste, the oldest type of preserved-tomato product, is a very useful flavoring agent for sauces. It must be diluted with liquid (water, usually) or it remains in lumps and throws off the balance of your sauce. Paste has a very pungent taste and only works in long-simmered sauces.

OLIVES

In the old days, olives meant little green things with a strip of red pepper where the pit used to be, and were most useful in martinis. Growing food awareness — especially with the spectacular popularity of olive oil — has brought olives to the fore as a foodstuff. They come in many varieties and all of them are tasty. In this book you'll find use for the green olives (the big green ones that come from Italy) and many recipes that call for black olives.

The best black olives, especially for cooking, are the withered ones, known variously as "oil-cured" and *arostiti* (roasted). They are packed with flavor and are very easy to pit, as they are soft. I recommend them highly.

CAPERS

Weird little berries, capers are sold in tiny size (from France), slightly larger (from Greece) and now, newly popular, ones that are the size of small grapes, actually known as "caper-berries." They are interchange-able in my recipes and add just the right tartness and flavor, especially with fish.

LEGUMES

Also known as beans, they are (along with "pulses") a primary source of protein for sunbelt areas where meagre grazing lands puts meat at a pre-mium. I use all kinds — white kidney, red Romano, black, as well as chickpeas, a bean relative. Beans need lengthy soaking and cooking, which means pre-planning. Luckily, they are all available in cans, which serve wonderfully as long as you strain and gently wash them to get rid of their "canned" taste. A normal can (19 oz [540 mL]) will yield the 2 cups [500 mL] of drained beans called for in the recipes.

PULSES (LENTILS)

These also come in many varieties. I use the green pea-sized ones, as well as the tiny red ones (called *dal* in India). Green lentils are available in cans, but they cook up so fast that I make them from scratch; with the red ones, there is no choice since they are not available canned. With both kinds, it is important to wash and drain them before using.

RICE

My preferred rice is the short-grain variety. It retains shape and texture after lengthy procedures better than long grain, and it has better taste. If you absolutely must use long grain, do so. It requires the same amount of moisture and in every respect responds to the recipes as written.

MEAT

The meat of choice for most Mediterranean food is lamb. It has the right texture and taste. On the other hand, there is no law that says you can't substitute pork or beef — feel free to do so if you don't like lamb or its cost (which can be considerable, especially in winter).

Many of my recipes call for 2 1/2 lbs (1.25 kg) of 1 1/2-inch (3 cm) chunks of lamb, bone in. This is a personal preference, since I like to carve meat from its bone, especially if from the "shoulder", with its extra gelatin and edible gristle. The recipes work perfectly well, however, with cubes of deboned lamb (or pork or beef) instead. Just use a lesser quan-tity: 1 1/4 to 1 1/2 lbs (675 to 750 g), cut into smaller 3/4-inch (2 cm) cubes. (This is the weight of the meat alone, without bones.)

CALAMARI

The popularity of calamari (or squid) has been driven largely by Greek restaurants, which fry it up so crunchily and defy us not to love it. With the gates open, we have also learned to love calamari grilled, poached, in seafood stews, in composed rice dishes (like paella) — you name it.

Calamari does offer some challenges. If purchased whole, squid requires major kitchen surgery to clean its innards and pull off its quill. There is also a bony structure attached to the ink sac at the base of the tentacles. For most uses, both ink sac and bony structure are best removed and discarded, a potentially messy business. Happily, most fishmongers offer calamari pre-cleaned and ready to use. Take up the offer.

VEGETABLES

There are many vegetables favored in Mediterranean cooking, but these are also used in most other cuisines and don't need discussion. There are, however, three special ones that require special mention:

Fennel: This delightful, licorice-flavored bulb has three parts: the spindly, dill-like leaves, which are very flavorful and can be used for garnish; the woody branches that stem out of the bulb (they're too fibrous, so cut them off and discard them); and, the bulb itself — the "business" part of the fennel, which has a hard core. To trim it, cut the bulb in quarters vertically. You'll see triangles of white, hard core inside each quarter. Cut these out and discard. Then proceed with the recipe.

Leeks: Oniony and sweet, leeks are full of nutrition and highly enjoyable. Their problem is the grit that hides where the white and green parts meet. The best way to deal with this grit (short of dismembering the leek altogether) is to make a deep lengthwise slit, about 3 inches (7.5 cm) long. This allows you to run cold water over the leek and to rub the grit off, while leaving it more-or-less intact, as required by the recipe. It is also a good idea to trim away the large green leaves near the bottom of the leek; cooked, they have an unpleasantly chewy texture.

Eggplant: This is the only vegetable I know that is utterly tasteless when raw, but combines exquisitely with oil and sauces to become a feast when cooked. Eggplant has several quirks, however, not the least of which is that it browns quickly when cut, so it must be salted, cooked or immersed in salted water immediately thereafter. Eggplant also has a certain bitterness, which somehow disappears when treated with salt. In my recipes I recommend that you salt eggplant if it is to be used in slices (and washed after) or that you cook it in salted water if it is to be used in salads or stews. Whole, it bakes into a royal purée, but it must be peeled, and its seed pods discarded after baking. It also tends to splutter wildly (and can injure) when fried in hot oil. But these are all minor matters. There is absolutely nothing that tastes quite like eggplant.

NUTS

All manner of nuts (with the possible exception of Macadamias) are used in Mediterranean cuisine — including the regal almond, walnuts, hazelnuts and, of course, those amazing pine nuts. All can be toasted in the oven, fried in oil, ground (either when toasted or raw) and usually skinned — although you won't necessarily find all these permutations available in grocery stores.

Toasting (or roasting) nuts is only a problem if you throw them in the oven and forget them. They're usually done within 10 to 15 minutes and they must be transferred to a cool plate when ready. (Nuts have been known to burn even out of the oven, just from the heat of a baking sheet.)

Grinding nuts is no longer the chore it once was, since every kitchen I know of has at least one device that can do the job (processor, blender, even a coffee grinder). Skinning nuts is another matter. If only skin-on nuts are available, your technique for skinning them will depend on the nut involved. Almonds are boiled for a second, and just slip out of their skins. Hazelnuts must be skinned after roasting — you rub them, the skins fall off and then you pick out the skinned nuts; or, even better, you take them outside, run a fan to blow away the skins and you're left with clean nuts. Walnuts have a very fine skin, and don't need to be skinned. And pine nuts, thankfully, come already skinned and ready to use.

SPICES

Every single spice known to cooking is used in the Mediterranean kitchen, which is only normal for a way of eating that was influenced so heavily by the cuisines of Asia. Most spices, whether sweet (cinnamon, nutmeg, allspice) or savory (cumin, coriander seeds, black pepper) are ground before using. Exceptions are fennel seeds, which melt in the cooking, as well as cloves, which are used whole. Saffron, the smoky, dusty, colorful (and expensive) spice from Spain and Greece is usually used in strands. All spices benefit from some sort of frying in the beginning of the cooking process; this releases their flavors and helps to make them more digestible.

CHILIES

This hot stuff is not as pervasive in the Mediterranean as it is in other sunbelt locations — such as Mexico or India — but it certainly has its place. You'll get the best effect from fresh chilies, though chili flakes or even cayenne can easily substitute. And if you can't take the heat? Feel free to omit the offending ingredients.

HERBS

The Mediterranean is essentially one big herb garden, with whole fields smelling of oregano, thyme or rosemary. Herbs are essential to all of these recipes and since many of them are cooked with the sauces, dried ones (used early in the cooking) are perfectly acceptable. However, using the fresh variety — of basil, coriander, dill or even parsley — as a final garnish will reward handsomely in terms of flavor, color and enjoyment.

Appetizers

Bitter Greens with Paprika   22

Mushroom and Green Bean Stir-Fry   23

Braised Green Beans and Fennel   24

Braised Endive and Tomato Gratinée   25

Sautéed Eggplant Salad   26

"Little" Broccoli Gratin   28

Wild Mushroom Fricassee   29

Portobello Mushrooms with Goat Cheese   30

Zucchini Croquettes with Yogurt Salad   32

Lentils with Spicy Sausage   34

Spicy Sausage Palaio Faliro   35

Grilled Leeks with Feta and Red Pepper   36

Bruschetta Tapenade   38

Goat Cheese Filo Nests with Cashews   40

Mint Feta Filo Nests   41

Asparagus and Scallops Gratin   42

Individual Asparagus and Goat Cheese
Flan   44

Saffron Scallops with Peach Butter   45

Crusted Cod with Cherry Tomatoes   46

Grilled Fresh Sardines with Red Onion
Sauce   48

BITTER GREENS WITH PAPRIKA

Suitable as a starter or as a side dish with grilled or roasted meat, this hyper-nutritious dish has taste to spare. Here the bitterness of the main ingredient merges meaningfully with the various aromatics and condiments. A whole new dimension can be achieved by using non-bitter greens — like collard or kale — with exactly the same enhancements, making this an all-season recipe for the greens of your choice.

1	bunch rapini or dandelion greens, washed, bottom 2 inches (5 cm) of stalks trimmed	1
2 tbsp	olive oil	25 mL
1 tsp	sweet paprika	5 mL
1/4 tsp	turmeric	1 mL
1/4 tsp	salt	1 mL
1/4 tsp	freshly ground black pepper	1 mL
3	cloves garlic, thinly sliced	3
2 tbsp	lemon juice	25 mL
1 tsp	drained capers	5 mL

1. Cut stalks of greens in half. Bring a pot of salted water to a boil and add the lower half of stalks. Let water return to boil and cook for 3 minutes. Add upper half of stalks (with the leaves); return to boil and cook for 3 minutes. Rinse under cold water; drain and set aside.

2. In a large frying pan, combine oil, paprika, turmeric, salt and pepper. Cook, stirring, over high heat for 1 minute. Add garlic; stir-fry for 30 seconds. Add drained greens; stir-fry for 2 minutes, folding from the bottom up to distribute garlic and spices evenly. Reduce heat to medium. Stir in lemon juice; cook, stirring, for 2 minutes. Stir in capers. Serve immediately.

MUSHROOM AND GREEN BEAN STIR-FRY

Mixing and matching vegetables to create delicious combinations is an age-old culinary trick to get healthy food on the table. The appeal of this one is derived from the crunchy mushrooms, which contrast so nicely with the tenderness of the green beans. The whole lot is enhanced by the aromatics and lemon juice. It makes for a light starter, or a perfect accompaniment to grilled meat or fish in a main course.

8 oz	green beans, trimmed and halved	250 g
4 oz	carrots, scraped and sliced into 1/4-inch (5 mm) rounds	125 g
1/4 cup	olive oil	50 mL
8 oz	mushrooms, trimmed and cut into 1/2-inch (1 cm) chunks	250 g
5	cloves garlic, thinly sliced	5
3	sun-dried tomatoes, thinly sliced	3
1/2 tsp	salt	2 mL
1/4 tsp	freshly ground black pepper	1 mL
2 tbsp	freshly squeezed lemon juice	25 mL
1/2 cup	white wine	125 mL
4	canned artichoke hearts, drained and cut into quarters	4
1/3 cup	roasted pine nuts	75 mL
	Extra virgin olive oil for drizzling (optional)	

1. Bring a pot of salted water to a boil. Add green beans and carrots; let water return to a boil and cook 5 minutes. Rinse under plenty of cold water; drain and set aside.

2. In a large frying pan, heat oil over high heat for 1 minute. Add mushrooms and cook, stirring actively, 3 minutes until golden brown on all sides (they will absorb all or most of the oil). Add garlic, sun-dried tomatoes, salt and pepper; stir-fry for 1 minute.

3. Immediately add lemon juice and let it sizzle for 1 minute. Stir in wine; bring to a boil and cook, stirring, for 1 minute. Reduce heat to medium-high. Add beans and carrots; cook, stirring, for 2 minutes. Add artichoke hearts; cook, stirring, for 3 minutes. Serve immediately, garnished with pine nuts and, if desired, with olive oil on the side for drizzling at table.

BRAISED GREEN BEANS AND FENNEL

SERVES 4 TO 6

Here's another healthy and interesting way to serve up Mediterranean-style vegetables. In this recipe we forego boiling in favor of a quick stir-fry followed by 20 minutes of braising and simmering. The result is a comfortingly soft, yet still crunchy texture, and a pleasing licorice flavor. The recipe works beautifully as a warm-up starter-salad, or as a side vegetable to grilled meat or fish. Green beans provide the bulk, but it is the fresh fennel that gives it character.

A note on fennel: The fennel bulb always comes attached to woody branches and thin leaves that look like dill. You'll need the leaves for the final garnish, so cut them off and set them aside. Cut off and discard the woody branches. Quarter the bulb vertically, then cut out and discard the hard triangular sections of core. What remains is the usable part of the fennel.

1/4 cup	olive oil	50 mL
1/2 tsp	salt	2 mL
1/4 tsp	freshly ground black pepper	1 mL
1 tsp	whole fennel seeds	5 mL
12 oz	green beans, trimmed	375 g
1	large (or 2 small) fennel bulbs, trimmed, cored, and cut into 1/2-inch (1 cm) slices	1
4 oz	carrots, scraped and sliced into 1/4-inch (5 mm) rounds	125 g
6	cloves garlic, thinly sliced	6
1 cup	water	250 mL
1 tbsp	balsamic vinegar	15 mL
	Few sprigs fennel greens, chopped	

1. In a large, deep frying pan, heat olive oil, salt and pepper over high heat for 1 minute. Add fennel seeds; stir-fry 1 minute or until just browning. Add green beans, fennel and carrots; stir-fry 3 minutes or until all the vegetables are shiny and beginning to sizzle. Add garlic; stir-fry for 1 more minute.

2. Immediately add water and vinegar; cook 2 minutes or until bubbling. Reduce heat to medium-low, cover pan tightly and cook 20 minutes.

3. Place a strainer over a bowl and strain contents of the pan. Transfer the strained vegetables onto a platter and keep warm. Transfer the liquid that has collected in the bowl back into the pan; bring to a boil and cook 6 to 7 minutes or until thick and syrupy.

4. Spoon the reduced sauce over the vegetables, garnish with the chopped fennel greens and serve immediately.

BRAISED ENDIVE AND TOMATO GRATINÉE

SERVES 2

The endive isn't particularly Mediterranean, but it's plentiful in our part of the world and it's available throughout the year. Here's a recipe that combines endive with sun-belt flavors and uses the ancient French culinary method of braising or slow cooking.

2	medium endives	2
2 tbsp	water	25 mL
1 tbsp	olive oil	15 mL
4	black olives, pitted and cut into thirds	4
2	cloves garlic, thinly sliced	2
2	sun-dried tomatoes, cut into thirds	2
1	ripe tomato, cut into 1/2-inch (1 cm) wedges	1
Pinch	dried oregano	Pinch
Pinch	dried basil	Pinch
1/4 tsp	salt	1 mL
1/8 tsp	freshly ground black pepper	0.5 mL
2 oz	sharp cheese (such as Pecorino, Parmesan or old Cheddar), shredded	50 g
	Few sprigs fresh basil or parsley, chopped	

1. Place endives into a small shallow pot with a lid. Add water, olive oil, olives, garlic, sun-dried tomatoes, tomato, oregano, basil, salt and pepper; cook over high heat for 1 to 2 minutes until bubbling. Push the tomato wedges to the bottom of the pot around the endives, pushing the other ingredients into the ensuing liquid. Reduce heat to minimum, cover and cook undisturbed for 35 minutes or until soft and pierceable. (The recipe can prepared to this point up to 2 hours in advance.)

2. Carefully transfer endives to a small ovenproof dish. (They should fit snuggly.) Cover endives with sauce. With a sharp knife, slice the endives halfway down and open up the cuts so that they are somewhat butterflied. Sprinkle shredded cheese evenly on the butterflied surfaces. Place under a hot broiler for 3 to 4 minutes, until the cheese is bubbling and beginning to char. Lift the endives carefully with a spatula onto 2 plates and pour sauce around them. Garnish with chopped basil or parsley. Serve immediately.

SAUTÉED EGGPLANT SALAD

SERVES 4

An oily pleasure, eggplant is such a joy to eat that we tend to forgive it all its excesses. A huge favorite in southern Europe (and all over the sunbelt), it appears in countless recipes. Our adaptation appears here, using ratatouille as a base and touching on the various stewed and sautéed eggplant salads of the Middle East. The chilies were an enhancement to please the "heat" requirements of the cast and crew of *Love! Valour! Compassion!*, whose filming we catered. If you like things less spicy, just omit the chili flakes.

4 cups	eggplant, cut into 1/2-inch (1 cm) cubes	1 L
	Salted water	
3 tbsp	vegetable oil	45 mL
3 tbsp	olive oil	45 mL
1/2 tsp	salt	2 mL
1/4 tsp	freshly ground black pepper	1 mL
1/4 tsp	chili flakes	1 mL
1	onion, cut into 1/4-inch (5 mm) slices	1
Half	green pepper, cut into 1/2-inch (1 cm) squares	Half
Half	red bell pepper, cut into 1/2-inch (1 cm) squares	Half
4	cloves garlic, thinly sliced	4
4	sun-dried tomatoes, thinly sliced	4
1	medium tomato, cut into 1/2-inch (1 cm) wedges	1
1 tsp	red wine vinegar	5 mL
1/2 tsp	dried basil	2 mL
1/2 tsp	dried oregano	2 mL
1/4 cup	water	50 mL
	Few sprigs chopped fresh basil and/or parsley	
	Grated Romano cheese	

1. Immerse cubed eggplant in cold salted water as soon as possible after cutting it (eggplant turns brown soon after it is cut); let soak 5 to 10 minutes

2. In a large nonstick frying pan, heat vegetable oil over medium-high heat for 1 minute. Drain eggplant and add to the pan (watch for splutters). It will absorb all the oil almost immediately. Cook, stirring actively for 6 to 7 minutes or until the eggplant is soft and browned all over. Transfer the cooked eggplant to a dish; set aside.

3. Using the same frying pan, heat olive oil over medium-high heat for 30 seconds. Add salt, pepper and chili flakes; stir-fry for 30 seconds. Add onion, green and red pepper; stir-fry 2 to 3 minutes or until wilted and beginning to char. Add garlic and sun-dried tomatoes; stir-fry 1 minute. Add tomato, vinegar, basil and oregano; stir-fry 2 minutes or until tomato has broken down and a sauce is forming. Add water and immediately reduce heat to medium. Stir in eggplant. Gently mix and fold all ingredients together; cook 2 minutes or until heated through.

4. Transfer to a flat dish and let rest for about 10 minutes. Garnish with fresh herbs and sprinkle with grated cheese. Serve lukewarm.

"LITTLE" BROCCOLI GRATIN

The "little" part of this recipe refers to a fine-chopping technique (borrowed from DANIAILE'S "LITTLE" CAULIFLOWER SALAD, see page 56) that enhances the taste and texture of broccoli. The result combines crunchily boiled bits of broccoli with a number of zesty ingredients, all smothered in the lean mildness of melted bocconcini cheese and studded with toasted walnut pieces. It works well on its own and even better as a side dish to accompany brolled meat or chicken. If you wish, replace the bocconcini with the same weight of mozzarella nuggets — cut 1/4 inch (1 cm) thick — for a slightly saltier result.

10-inch (25 cm) pie plate or baking dish
Preheat broiler

1	bunch broccoli	1
2 tbsp	olive oil	25 mL
1/2 tsp	salt	2 mL
1/4 tsp	freshly ground black pepper	1 mL
1 tbsp	minced fresh chili pepper *or* 1/4 tsp (1 mL) chili flakes	15 mL
1 cup	thickly sliced red onions	250 mL
8 oz	button mushrooms, trimmed and halved	250 g
1 tbsp	raisins	15 mL
1 tsp	white wine vinegar	5 mL
8 oz	bocconcini cheese, cut into 1/4-inch (1 cm) rounds	250 g
1/2 cup	walnut pieces	125 mL

1. Separate florets of broccoli from the large stalks. (Reserve stalks for another use.) Chop florets into tiny match-head-sized bits. (You should get just over 2 cups [500 mL].) Bring a pot of salted water to a boil. Add broccoli; bring back to boil and cook for about 2 minutes. Drain through a fine wire strainer. Rinse under cold water; drain well and set aside.

2. In a large frying pan, heat oil, salt and pepper over high heat for 1 minute. Add chilies, onions and mushrooms; stir-fry for 3 minutes or until vegetables start to brown. Add raisins and vinegar; cook, stirring, for 30 seconds. Stir in broccoli; remove from heat.

3. Transfer contents of frying pan to a pie plate, spreading evenly to make a flat layer about 1/2 inch (1 cm) deep. Place rounds of bocconcini on top so that most of the surface is covered. Sprinkle the walnut pieces over the uncovered spots.

4. Broil 3 to 4 minutes until the cheese is melted and the walnuts have turned dark brown. Serve immediately in its baking dish to be portioned at table.

WILD MUSHROOM FRICASSEE WITH ROSEMARY

SERVES 2

When it comes to appetizers, there's no ingredient to match wild mushrooms — meaty, lean, digestible and memorably delicious all at once. Here's a recipe with which to dazzle lovers and others (it can be easily multiplied as long as you use a large enough frying pan). It takes minutes to prepare and is also adaptable: You can make it with either red or white wine, whatever you happen to have on hand — just be sure to use the same color vinegar as your wine. You can use any kind of wild mushroom you prefer. Oyster and shiitakes can be used whole, trimmed of tough stalks. Portobellos must also be trimmed, then cut into slices 1/2 inch (1 cm) thick. If your waistline allows, use an extra tablespoon (15 mL) of butter at the beginning, as well as the optional teaspoon (5 mL) at the end, for a taste sensation worthy of the finest restaurant.

1 tbsp	butter	15 mL
1 tbsp	olive oil	15 mL
Pinch	freshly ground black pepper	Pinch
1 cup	thickly sliced red onions	250 mL
6 oz	wild mushrooms, trimmed	175 g
1 tbsp	minced garlic	15 mL
1 tbsp	finely chopped fresh rosemary (or 1 tsp [5 mL] dried crumbled)	15 mL
Pinch	salt	Pinch
1/2 tsp	white or red wine vinegar	2 mL
1/2 cup	white or red wine	125 mL
1 tsp	butter (optional)	5 mL
2	slices whole-wheat or black bread, toasted	2
	Few sprigs fresh parsley, chopped	

1. In a large nonstick frying pan, heat 1 tbsp (15 mL) butter, oil and black pepper over high heat for 1 minute or until sizzling. Add onions and mushrooms; cook 3 to 4 minutes, turning every minute or so until they are nicely browned all over and have absorbed most of the liquid.

2. Add garlic and rosemary; stir-fry for 1 minute. Immediately add salt and vinegar; toss for a few seconds. Add wine and cook, shaking pan occasionally, for 2 to 3 minutes or until the sauce is thick and partially absorbed. Add optional 1 tsp (5 mL) butter and mix in until melted. Remove from heat.

3. Immediately cut the toasted bread diagonally into 4 pieces; arrange on 2 plates as toast points. Distribute mushrooms evenly in the middle of each plate and garnish with parsley. Serve immediately with a glass of the same wine you used in the recipe.

PORTOBELLO MUSHROOMS WITH GOAT CHEESE

SERVES 2

Exotic-sounding name notwithstanding, portobello mushrooms are nothing more than overgrown regular mushrooms. But for some alchemical reason their taste is very different (more meaty) from those lowly buttons. As a result they are usually associated with "wild" (or "fancy") mushrooms and are very much in demand. Luckily, they are available everywhere and often, quite conveniently, already trimmed and sliced into attractive 1/2-inch (1 cm) slices.

Green peppercorns are sold packed in brine; leftovers will keep if refrigerated in their original brine. While optional, they are delicious in this recipe.

Baking sheet
Preheat broiler

2 tbsp	olive oil	25 mL
6 oz	portobello mushrooms, trimmed and sliced 1/2 inch (1 cm) thick	175 g
1 tbsp	finely chopped garlic	15 mL
2 tsp	balsamic vinegar	10 mL
1/4 tsp	salt	1 mL
1/8 tsp	freshly ground black pepper	0.5 mL
1/4 tsp	drained green peppercorns (optional)	1 mL
2 oz	goat cheese	50 g
2 tsp	pine nuts	10 mL
	Several lettuce leaves	
2 tsp	olive oil	10 mL

1. In a nonstick frying pan, heat 2 tbsp (25 mL) olive oil over high heat for 1 minute. Add mushroom slices in one layer; cook 2 to 3 minutes or until nicely browned (they will absorb all the oil). Turn and cook second side for under a minute. Add garlic, 1 tsp (5 mL) of the balsamic vinegar, salt and pepper; continue cooking for 1 minute to brown the garlic somewhat.

2. Remove from heat. Arrange on baking sheet in 2 flat piles about 3 inches (7.5 cm) wide. Sprinkle evenly with green peppercorns, if using. Divide the goat cheese in two; make each half into a thick disc, about 1 inch (2.5 cm) wide. Place a disc of cheese on each pile of mushrooms. Sprinkle the pine nuts evenly over the piles, some on the cheese and some on the surrounding mushrooms. (The recipe can wait at this point up to 1 hour, covered and unrefrigerated).

3. Broil the mushrooms for just under 4 minutes or until the cheese is soft and a little brown, and the pine nuts are dark brown.

4. Line 2 plates with lettuce. Carefully lift each pile off the baking sheet and transfer as intact as possible onto the lettuce. Sprinkle about 1 tsp (5 mL) olive oil and 1/2 tsp (2 mL) balsamic vinegar over each portion and serve immediately.

ZUCCHINI CROQUETTES WITH YOGURT SALAD

**MAKES 48,
SERVING 8**

Notwithstanding the army of nutritional zealots apparently bent on eliminating it from our diets, deep-fried food is still the number-one party favorite. This particular item — juicy and flavorful on the inside, crispy and crunchy on the outside — is not without virtue, however: It absorbs very little oil and is composed primarily of shredded zucchini, a very healthy vegetable. It was always a hit at my mother's feast-day buffets in Istanbul, and has continued to play a significant role in my own holiday entertaining. The yogurt salad that accompanies the croquettes can be enjoyed with a number of other dishes — essentially, anything that benefits from a refreshing side course.

Yogurt Salad

1 cup	yogurt	250 mL
1	2-inch (5 cm) piece English cucumber, finely diced	1
2	green onions, finely chopped	2
1	medium tomato, seeded and finely diced	1
1/2 tsp	salt	2 mL
1/2 tsp	cayenne pepper	2 mL
1 tbsp	lemon juice	15 mL
1 tsp	extra virgin olive oil	5 mL

Zucchini Croquettes

1 lb	zucchini	500 g
1/4 cup	chopped fresh mint *or* dill	50 mL
1/2 cup	all-purpose flour	125 mL
1 tsp	salt	5 mL
1 tsp	freshly ground black pepper	5 mL
1/2 tsp	ground nutmeg	2 mL
4 oz	sharp cheese (such as Pecorino, Crotonese, old Cheddar), shredded	125 g
2	eggs, beaten	2
2 to 3 cups	vegetable oil	500 to 750 mL

1. Make the yogurt salad: In a bowl stir together yogurt, cucumber, green onions, tomato, salt and cayenne. Add lemon juice and olive oil; mix well. If using soon, cover and save unrefrigerated. If not, refrigerate (up to several hours), but let come to room temperature before serving.

2. Make the zucchini croquettes: In another bowl, shred zucchini through the largest holes of a grater. Stir in mint. Sift flour into bowl and mix in. Stir in salt, pepper, nutmeg and cheese. Add eggs and fold-mix just until all the liquid appears to be absorbed.

Recipe continues...

MINT FETA PHYLLO NESTS (PAGE 41) ➤

3. In a large pot or wok, add vegetable oil to a depth of 1 inch (2.5 cm). Heat to 325° F (160° C) on a deep-fry thermometer. (If you don't have a thermometer, heat oil over medium-high heat; test by adding a bit of croquette batter: it should sizzle and rise.) Add croquette batter in 2-tbsp (25 mL) dollops; add as many as the pot can accommodate without them touching one another. Fry 2 minutes per side or until crisp and browned, Drain on paper towels. Repeat procedure with remaining batter.

4. It is best to set out the yogurt sauce and let guests eat the croquettes as soon as they are cooked, with spoonfuls of the yogurt on the side. If you must fry them all before serving, keep the early batches warm in a low oven and serve as soon as the last ones are ready.

< MOROCCAN GRAPEFRUIT AND OLIVE SALAD (PAGE 59)

LENTILS WITH SPICY SAUSAGE

North Americans are finally acknowledging the lowly lentil for the miracle food that it is. Not only total protein nutrition, but also delicious and endlessly adaptable, with a slew of tasty recipes to choose from. Here's a winter-type lentil that can make either for a good entree on its own, or a hearty main course served with boiled potato and green salad. The butter enhancement is optional if it offends calorie-wise, but it will obviously add a welcome richness to the proceedings.

1 cup	green lentils	250 mL
4 cups	boiling water	1 L
4 or 5	cloves garlic, sliced	4 or 5
1	bay leaf	1
1/2 tsp	dried thyme	2 mL
1/4 tsp	freshly ground black pepper	1 mL
8 oz	spicy sausage (merguez, chorizo or spicy Italian)	250 g
1/2 cup	sliced onions	125 mL
1 tbsp	butter (optional)	15 mL
1 tsp	white wine vinegar	5 mL
	Salt to taste	
	Several sprigs fresh parsley, chopped	

1. In a pot soak lentils in 2 cups (500 mL) of the boiling water for 20 minutes. (Lentils will swell up and absorb most of the water.) Add remaining 2 cups (500 mL) boiling water; stir in the garlic, bay leaf, thyme and pepper. Cook, uncovered, over medium heat for 30 minutes, stirring very occasionally. At the end of this period the lentils should be tender but still holding their shape; if too much water has boiled off (there should be enough moisture to give a saucy appearance to the lentils), add 1/2 to 1 cup (125 to 250 mL) more water as needed.

2. Meanwhile, broil sausages and onions 3 to 4 minutes on each side. (They should not cook through; neither should the onions burn.) Remove and slice the sausages into 1/2-inch (1 cm) pieces. Set aside sausages and onions together.

3. When the lentils are done, transfer them to an ovenproof dish. Add butter(if using), vinegar and salt. Stir to mix. Add sausages and onions; stir until well distributed. Bake uncovered in a preheated 400° F (200° C) oven for 30 minutes. Serve immediately garnished with chopped fresh parsley.

SPICY SAUSAGES PALAIO FALIRO

SERVES 4

Tired of the same old grilled sausage sitting unadorned on your plate? This variation dresses up sausage with aromatics and a mustard-balsamic sauce, which I first encountered in the seaside Athenian suburb of Palaio Faliro, an expatriate community of my fellow Istanbul Greeks where "food with gusto" (an Istanbul obsession) came along with the diaspora. Italian sausage works best here; it's available in most supermarkets. I recommend the spicy variety because I'm from Istanbul and like things perky. But if you're spice-shy, the sweet Italian sausage works just as well.

Preheat broiler or grill

1 tbsp	balsamic vinegar	15 mL
1 tsp	Dijon mustard	5 mL
2 tbsp	extra virgin olive oil	25 mL
1 lb	Italian sausage (spicy or sweet)	500 g
1/4 cup	thinly sliced red onions	50 mL
1/4 cup	thinly sliced strips green peppers	50 mL
	Several tomato wedges	
	Few sprigs fresh parsley, chopped	

1. In a small bowl, combine vinegar and mustard, stirring until smooth. Add olive oil and set aside, covered.

2. Add sausages to a pot of boiling water. Reduce heat to medium and cook, uncovered, 7 to 8 minutes or until firm to the touch.

3. Grill or broil sausages on high heat for 3 to 4 minutes each side or until charred on both sides. Remove from heat; immediately slice sausages into 1/2 inch (1 cm) rounds — preferably cutting on the diagonal, which will make a better presentation.

4. Portion out sausage pieces onto 4 plates. Stir sauce and drizzle equal amounts of it on the sausages. Garnish with red onions, green peppers, tomatoes and parsley. Serve immediately while still hot.

GRILLED LEEKS WITH FETA AND RED PEPPER

It is rumored that the laborers who built the pyramids of ancient Egypt survived primarily on leeks (cooked in honey, but that's another story). If true, that tidbit of leek-lore should put this oniony, versatile vegetable in league with Popeye's spinach. Its superpowers aside, the leek is a lovely vegetable and easy to deal with, if certain care is taken — especially with cleaning. The final presentation of this recipe depends for its beauty on the leek being cooked (using 2 separate techniques consecutively) with its stem intact so that it can stay in one long, graceful piece. The slit required in Step 1 is also tricky, since it has to be wide and deep enough to allow cleaning but without slicing right through.

13- by 9-inch (3 L) baking dish
Preheat broiler

4	leeks (about 1 lb [500 g])	4
1/4 cup	olive oil	50 mL
1	red bell pepper, trimmed and quartered	1
4 oz	feta cheese, crumbled	125 g
1 tbsp	red wine vinegar	15 mL
1/4 tsp	freshly ground black pepper	1 mL
4	black olives, pitted and chopped	4

1. To ensure that leeks do not separate, cut a 3-inch (7.5 cm) slit lengthwise through the middle of each leek. Wash sand away from central layers (where the white and green meet) through this slit. Bring a large pot of salted water to a boil. Add leeks; cook 6 to 8 minutes or until tender and easily pierceable. Drain. Rinse with cold water; drain.

2. Spread 1 tbsp (15 mL) of the olive oil in the bottom of baking dish. Transfer the leeks onto the oil and straighten them to their original length. Roll them in the oil, ending with the slit-side up. Fit the red pepper quarters into the corners of the pan and roll, coating both sides in the oil, ending with skin-side up. Mound one-quarter of the feta crumbles into the slit cavity of each leek and spread it out to cover the length of the slit. (The recipe can be prepared to this point and kept up to 1 hour, covered and unrefrigerated).

3. Broil leeks under a hot broiler for 7 to 10 minutes or until the feta is browned and the peppers are quite charred.

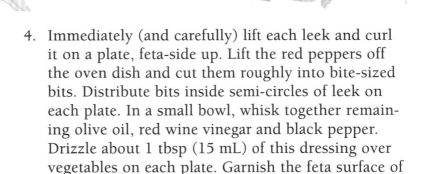

4. Immediately (and carefully) lift each leek and curl it on a plate, feta-side up. Lift the red peppers off the oven dish and cut them roughly into bite-sized bits. Distribute bits inside semi-circles of leek on each plate. In a small bowl, whisk together remaining olive oil, red wine vinegar and black pepper. Drizzle about 1 tbsp (15 mL) of this dressing over vegetables on each plate. Garnish the feta surface of the leeks with olive bits and serve immediately while still warm.

Bruschetta Tapenade

Originally, bruschetta was nothing more than toasted bread doused in olive oil and flavored with a herb (most notably fresh rosemary). Nowadays bruschetta, like its cousin pizza, is cropping up with a variety of interesting toppings, making it suitable as an opening course instead of a mere accompaniment. Here we join the fray and offer this bruschetta, topped with tapenade (olive dip), vegetables and cheese, then baked. The only variable here is the kind of olives you use — the milder your olive, the sweeter your tapenade. The best bread to use is a large white Italian loaf, which bakes crispy and surrenders its own mild taste to that of your topping ingredients.

Large baking sheet
Preheat oven to 375° F (190° C)

Tapenade

20	black olives, pitted and quartered	20
2 tbsp	extra virgin olive oil	25 mL
1 tsp	balsamic vinegar	5 mL
1 tbsp	drained capers	15 mL
2	anchovies, minced	2
1 tsp	finely minced garlic	5 mL
1/2 tsp	dried thyme	2 mL
1/4 tsp	freshly ground black pepper	1 mL

Bruschetta

8	slices white Italian bread, 1/2 inch (1 cm) thick and 5 inches (12.5 cm) across	8
1 tbsp	olive oil	15 mL
1	zucchini, sliced paper thin (about 8 oz [250 g])	1
6	plum tomatoes, finely diced (about 12 oz [375 g]), with juice	6
8 oz	mozzarella cheese, shredded	250 g
1 tbsp	grated Romano cheese	15 mL
	Few sprigs fresh basil and parsley, chopped	

1. In a food processor combine olives, oil, vinegar, capers, anchovies, garlic, thyme and pepper. Pulse on and off 6 or 7 times, scraping down sides of bowl, until well mixed with a coarse texture. Set aside.

2. Lightly brush one side of the bread with olive oil. Put on baking sheet, oiled side down. Spread a thin layer of tapenade on the bread, covering all the surface (you should have just enough tapenade). Lay out slices of zucchini on the tapenade, and bits of tomato over the zucchini. Top with shredded mozzarella and a light sprinkling of grated Romano.

3. Bake for 15 minutes or until the cheese has melted and bottoms of the bread are golden. Place 2 slices per plate and garnish with chopped herbs. Serve immediately.

GOAT CHEESE PHYLLO NESTS WITH CASHEWS

SERVES 4

Phyllo is a magic ingredient. If properly deployed (oiled between each layer), it rewards with a festive look and is perfect for any party. Here, with the help of a muffin tin, we create frilly "nests" stuffed with a flavored goat cheese and topped with cashews.

12-cup muffin tin, 8 of the cups lightly oiled
Preheat oven to 350° F (180° C)

6 oz	softened goat cheese	175 g
2	eggs, beaten	2
1/4 cup	chopped fresh parsley	50 mL
4	green olives, pitted and chopped	4
1/2 tsp	salt	2 mL
1/4 tsp	freshly ground black pepper	1 mL
6	large sheets phyllo dough	6
1/4 cup	olive oil	50 mL
16	roasted unsalted whole cashews (about 2 oz [50 g])	16

1. Mix goat cheese and eggs until combined but still lumpy. (There should be little bits of unmelted cheese in the mixture.) Stir in parsley, green olives, salt (use less, depending on the saltiness of the goat cheese) and pepper. Cover and refrigerate at least 30 minutes. (This will allow for easier handling.)

2. On a dry surface, layer 3 sheets of phyllo on top of one another, lightly brushing with olive oil between layers. Brush top surface with oil. Cut the layered phyllo into quarters. Carefully lift each quarter and gently fit into the middle of an oiled muffin cup, fluting the edges that rise off the cup to resemble a nest. Repeat layering-cutting-nest-building procedure with remaining 3 phyllo sheets to produce a total of 8 nests.

3. Spoon one-eighth of cheese mixture (about 2 tbsp [25 mL]) into each nest. Top each with 2 cashews.

4. Bake undisturbed for 20 minutes or until phyllo is golden brown and the cheese filling has set. Remove from oven and let rest for 10 minutes. Unmold from the muffin tin (they'll slip off easily). Serve 2 nests per person.

MINT FETA PHYLLO NESTS

SERVES 4

In this variation on the previous recipe, we use less expensive feta with a minty twist. The sharp-tasting 3-to-1 ratio of feta to mozzarella can be mellowed by using equal portions (4 oz [125 g]) of each cheese. And if you're using fresh mint (which we heartily recommend), feel free to double the quantity called for in the recipe.

12-cup muffin tin, 8 of the cups lightly oiled
Preheat oven to 350° F (180° C)

6 oz	feta cheese, crumbled	175 g
1/2 cup	shredded mozzarella (about 2 oz [50 g])	125 mL
3 tbsp	minced red onions	45 mL
2 tbsp	minced red bell peppers	25 mL
1 tsp	olive oil	5 mL
Pinch	cayenne pepper	Pinch
1/4 cup	chopped fresh mint (or 1 tbsp [15 mL] dried)	50 mL
2	eggs, beaten	2
6	sheets phyllo dough	6
1/4 cup	olive oil	50 mL

1. In a bowl with a fork, mash feta with mozzarella until well crumbled and mixed together. Set aside.

2. In a small nonstick saucepan, combine red onions, red peppers, 1 tsp (5 mL) olive oil and the cayenne pepper. Cook over medium-high heat, stirring, for 4 minutes or until softened but not browned. Remove from heat; stir into cheese mixture. Stir in mint and eggs until well mixed. Cover bowl and refrigerate at least 20 minutes or up to 24 hours.

3. On a dry surface, layer 3 sheets of phyllo on top of one another, lightly brushing with olive oil between layers. Brush top surface with oil. Cut the layered phyllo into quarters. Carefully lift each quarter and gently fit into the middle of an oiled muffin cup, fluting the edges that rise off the cup to resemble a nest. Repeat layering-cutting-nest-building procedure with remaining 3 phyllo sheets to produce a total of 8 nests.

4. Spoon one-eighth of cheese mixture (about 3 tbsp [45 mL]) into each nest.

5. Bake undisturbed for 20 minutes or until phyllo is golden brown and the cheese filling has set. Remove from oven and let rest for 10 minutes. Unmold from the muffin tin (they'll slip off easily). Serve 2 nests per person.

ASPARAGUS AND SCALLOPS GRATIN

SERVES 4

It is always a challenge to discover interesting ways to cook up bay scallops — those inexpensive little dollops of sea-sweetness that can't quite match the elegance of the larger and very pricey, regular scallops, but taste just as wonderful. Here's an invented recipe that combines them with asparagus and tomatoes for an appetizer that seems novel, but delivers comfort with its combination of compatible aromatics.

Four 1 1/2-cup (375 mL) ramekins, about 4 inches (10 cm) across and 1 1/2 inches (4 cm) deep
Baking sheet
Preheat broiler

1 lb	asparagus (about 24 stems), bottom 1 1/2 inches (4 cm) trimmed	500 g
3 tbsp	olive oil	45 mL
1/2 tsp	salt	2 mL
1/4 tsp	freshly ground black pepper	1 mL
1 tbsp	finely chopped garlic	15 mL
1 tbsp	grated lemon zest	15 mL
2	sun-dried tomatoes, finely chopped	2
2 cups	tomatoes, peeled and cut into 1/2-inch (1 cm) cubes, with juice *or* canned tomatoes	500 mL
1 tbsp	lemon juice	15 mL
1 tsp	dried tarragon	5 mL
1/4 cup	breadcrumbs	50 mL
8 oz	bay scallops	250 g
	Few sprigs fresh tarragon or parsley, chopped	

1. Bring a large pot of water to a boil. Add trimmed asparagus, return to a boil and cook for 3 minutes. Drain. Rinse under cold water; drain. Cut into 1-inch (2.5 cm) pieces; set aside.

2. In a large frying pan, heat 2 tbsp (25 mL) of the olive oil with salt and pepper for 30 seconds over high heat. Add garlic, lemon zest and sun-dried tomatoes; stir-fry for 1 minute or until starting to brown. Add tomatoes, lemon juice and tarragon; cook, stirring, for 1 minute or until sizzling. Reduce heat to medium and cook, stirring for 2 to 3 minutes or until the tomatoes have broken down and a sauce has formed. Stir in reserved asparagus pieces and remove from heat.

3. Divide asparagus and sauce between ramekins. Sprinkle each with 1 tbsp (15 mL) of the breadcrumbs, pushing breadcrumbs slightly into the sauce. (Recipe can be prepared to this point up to 2 hours ahead; keep covered and unrefrigerated.)

4. Rinse and drain the scallops; transfer to a bowl. Sprinkle with remaining olive oil; roll them in the olive oil until completely coated. Place one-quarter of the scallops on top of the breadcrumbs in each ramekin.

5. Broil 6 to 7 minutes or until scallops feel firm to the touch and the breadcrumbs have started to brown. Do not unmold. Serve immediately in the ramekins, garnished with chopped herbs.

INDIVIDUAL ASPARAGUS AND GOAT CHEESE FLAN

SERVES 4

Asparagus is the most elegant of vegetables and, happily for us, it is available year-round. In the south of France, where they only eat it in season (spring), they make a delicious omelette with the thinnest stalks. Here's a take on their omelettes which works with any size asparagus you can find. It ends up saucy and tart — a perfect appetizer for a dinner party.

Four 1/2-cup (125 mL) ramekins
Baking sheet
Preheat oven to 400° F (200° C)

1 lb	asparagus (about 24 stems), bottom 1 1/2 inches (4 cm) trimmed	500 g
4 oz	softened goat cheese	125 g
2	eggs, beaten	2
2	green onions, chopped into 1/4-inch (5 mm) pieces	2
1 tbsp	lemon juice	15 mL
1/4 tsp	salt	1 mL
1/4 tsp	freshly ground black pepper	1 mL
1 tsp	olive oil	5 mL
2 tbsp	pine nuts	25 mL

1. Bring a large pot of water to a boil. Add trimmed asparagus, return to a boil and cook for 3 minutes. Drain. Rinse under cold water; drain. Cut into 1 1/2-inch (4 cm) pieces; set aside.

2. In a bowl mix goat cheese with eggs until combined but still lumpy. Stir in asparagus, green onions, lemon juice, salt and pepper. Brush bottom of ramekins with oil. Divide asparagus mixture between ramekins; sprinkle evenly with pine nuts.

3. Transfer ramekins to baking sheet. Bake 15 to 18 minutes or until set around edges but still slightly runny just at the center. Do not unmold. Serve immediately in ramekins.

SAFFRON SCALLOPS WITH PEACH BUTTER

SERVES 4

Nouvelle cuisine has become notorious for its excessive use of fruit in sauces and garnishes — so much so that all of us who enjoy certain fruits in selected recipes have run for cover. Nevertheless, we've had such success with this dish during our movie-catering days that we dare to offer it. A summery combination of ripe peaches and affordable bay scallops, slightly smoky with saffron, and accented with a little lemon-tartness. It's irresistible for seafood lovers — especially if you avoid the temptation to overcook the scallops.

8 oz	bay scallops	250 g
1/4 cup	all-purpose flour	50 mL
2 tbsp	olive oil	25 mL
1/4 tsp	salt	1 mL
1/8 tsp	freshly ground black pepper	0.5 mL
1 tbsp	butter	15 mL
12 oz	ripe peaches (about 3), peeled and cut into sixths	375 g
Pinch	saffron threads	Pinch
1 tsp	lemon juice	5 mL
1/4 cup	finely chopped green onions	50 mL
1/2 cup	fish stock *or* chicken stock *or* white wine	125 mL
4	lettuce leaves	4
1/4 cup	finely diced red bell peppers	50 mL
	Lemon wedges	

1. Rinse and drain the scallops. Toss with flour to coat; transfer to a strainer and shake of excess flour. In a large nonstick frying pan, heat oil with salt and pepper over high heat for 1 minute. Add scallops; cook 2 to 3 minutes, turning, until lightly browned on all sides. With a slotted spoon, transfer scallops to a bowl, leaving as much oil as possible in the pan; set scallops aside.

2. Return pan to high heat. Add butter; when melted, add peaches, saffron, lemon juice and most of the green onions. Cook, stirring, 1 minute. Add fish stock; cook, stirring, 1 minute or until peaches are very soft and sauce is bubbling. Reduce heat to medium. Stir in scallops and any liquid that has accumulated; cook, stirring, for 1 minute. Remove from heat.

3. Line 4 plates with lettuce leaves. Portion out the scallops, peaches and sauce. Garnish with red peppers and remainder of the green onions. Garnish with a lemon wedge on the side and serve immediately.

CRUSTED COD WITH CHERRY TOMATOES

Cod is an ancient fish that, whether fresh or salted and dried, has graced the palate of the Mediterranean peoples for millennia. The problem with fresh cod is that it flakes easily and separates when cooked. The solution? Bread the fish, then fry it. Here we use a crust of colorfully spiced cornmeal and fry it in just a little oil (thanks to the magic of nonstick frying pans). It is an airy starter course for a serious supper, and is especially appealing with its accompanying fried cherry tomatoes.

1/4 cup	yellow cornmeal	50 mL
1 tsp	sweet paprika	5 mL
1/2 tsp	turmeric	2 mL
12 oz	skinless boneless fresh cod fillet, cut into 4 equal chunks	375 g
1/4 cup	olive oil	50 mL
1/2 tsp	salt	2 mL
1/4 tsp	freshly ground black pepper	1 mL
1/2 cup	thinly sliced red onions	125 mL
1 tbsp	lemon zest, cut into strips	15 mL
12	cherry tomatoes	12
1 tsp	dried oregano	5 mL
3 tbsp	lemon juice	45 mL
	Few sprigs fresh parsley, chopped	
	Lemon wedges	

1. Put cornmeal on a plate and stir paprika and turmeric into it, until more-or-less combined. Roll cod chunks in the cornmeal to dredge well; set aside. (Discard leftover cornmeal.)

2. In a large nonstick frying pan, heat 2 tbsp (25 mL) of the oil for 1 minute over high heat. Add dredged cod; cook each side for 2 to 3 minutes until golden and firm to the touch (flip carefully, so as not to break up the cod). Take off heat and transfer cod to 4 warmed plates. Cover with foil to keep warm.

3. Working quickly, wipe the frying pan clean and place it on medium-high heat. Add remaining oil, salt and pepper; heat for 30 seconds. Add red onions and lemon zest; stir-fry for 1 minute or until softened. Add cherry tomatoes and oregano; stir-fry for 2 minutes or until tomatoes threaten to burst. Stir in lemon juice; cook for 30 seconds. Remove from heat.

4. Put 3 cherry tomatoes on the side of each piece of cod; top fish with onions and a spare drizzling of sauce. Garnish with chopped parsley and lemon wedges. Serve immediately.

GRILLED FRESH SARDINES WITH RED ONION SAUCE

For most North Americans, sardines are rarely seen in any form other than canned. Fortunately for those of us who live in cities with sizable Greek and Portuguese communities, however, we can now find local fish mongers who regularly fly fresh sardines in from Greece and Portugal. Of course, if you manage to locate fresh sardines (frozen ones aren't worth it) you may be put off by the prospect of preparing the little creatures for cooking on the grill. Gutting them is, admittedly, a bit bloody and messy, but the sardines' transparent scales actually come off easily with a wipe of the paper towel. So don't be intimidated. A charcoal-grilled fresh sardine is one of gastronomy's greatest thrills.

Note: A grilled sardine is not unlike a bone-in canned sardine. The top layer comes off the bone easily and then the bone comes off in one piece to reveal the bottom layer.

Preheat grill or broiler

1 lb	fresh sardines (about 8 to 12), gutted, scaled, gently washed and dried	500 g
4 tbsp	extra virgin olive oil	60 mL
2 tbsp	finely chopped fresh parsley	25 mL
2 tbsp	minced red onions	25 mL
1 tbsp	lemon juice	15 mL
Pinch	cayenne pepper	Pinch
	Salt and pepper to taste	

1. Put the sardines in a deep plate. Sprinkle with 1 tbsp (15 mL) of the olive oil; roll sardines around until thoroughly oiled. Cover and set aside, unrefrigerated, for 10 to 15 minutes.

2. In a small bowl, combine parsley, red onions, lemon juice, remaining olive oil, cayenne, salt and pepper. Set aside.

3. Grill (preferably a flip-grill for easy turning) or broil the sardines for 2 to 3 minutes each side, until firm to the touch and somewhat charred. Serve with the sauce on the side for spooning at table.

Salads

Lettuce and Avocado Salad   50

Warm Salad with Shallots   51

Arugula-Bocconcini Salad   52

Greek Bean and Tomato Salad   53

Istanbul Leeks   54

Summer Artichoke Salad   55

Daniaile's "Little" Cauliflower Salad   56

Potato and Tuna Salad   58

Morrocan Grapefruit and Olive Salad   59

Jane's Chicken Salad   60

Italian Squid Salad   62

Smoked Salmon and Avocado Salad   63

Marinated Salmon with Red Onion and
Crème Fraîche   64

Mixed Peppers and Seafood Salad   66

Lobster Salad   68

LETTUCE AND AVOCADO SALAD

SERVES 4

As non-traditional produce begins to appear in their markets, the Greeks are just now discovering the joys of avocado. It won't be long before they begin to incorporate this buttery fruit into their salads. And let us be the first to suggest a marriage of lettuce, feta cheese and avocado for a salad that works in summer as well as winter. We have reduced the quantity of olive oil to account for the richness of the avocado.

8 cups	lettuce (any variety), washed, dried and torn into bite-size pieces	2 L
4	green onions, chopped	4
1 tsp	drained capers	5 mL
	Few sprigs fresh coriander, roughly chopped	
2	ripe avocados	2
1/4 tsp	salt	1 mL
1/4 tsp	freshly ground black pepper	1 mL
2 tbsp	white wine vinegar	25 mL
4 oz	feta cheese, crumbled in large chunks	125 g
2 tbsp	extra virgin olive oil	25 mL

1. In a salad bowl, toss together lettuce, green onions, capers and coriander. Peel and slice (or scoop) avocado and add to lettuce. Immediately add salt and pepper; sprinkle vinegar all over the avocado (to avoid discoloration). Toss well to combine.

2. Add feta crumbles and drizzle olive oil over everything. Toss well, getting as much as possible of the feta back on top. Serve within 10 to 15 minutes.

WARM SALAD WITH SHALLOTS

SERVES 4

Often confused with green onions (in misused name only), shallots are those miniature red onion-type bulbs that always lurk near the onion and garlic section of vegetable counters. Greatly appreciated by the French in salad dressings and sauces for oysters, the magic of the shallot really shines through when combined with the pungency of vinegar. Here, we present a caramelized version that minimally but elegantly dresses lettuce, wilting it ever so slightly, making it a beautifully summer salad that is also suitable for winter. The addition of a few pieces of bocconcini or fresh mozzarella adds substance to the dish if it is served alone as a starter. Without the cheese, it serves admirably as an accompaniment to a main course.

8 cups	lettuce, washed, dried and torn to bite-size pieces	2 L
Half	red bell pepper, cut into thin strips	Half
2 oz	bocconcini or fresh mozzarella (optional) cut into 1/2-inch (1 cm) cubes	50 g
1/4 cup	olive oil	50 mL
1/2 tsp	salt	2 mL
1/4 tsp	freshly ground black pepper	1 mL
1/2 cup	thinly sliced shallots	125 mL
2	cloves garlic, thinly sliced	2
2 tbsp	balsamic vinegar	25 mL
12	cherry tomatoes	12

1. In a salad bowl, toss together lettuce, red pepper and cheese (if using); set aside.
2. In a small frying pan, heat oil with salt and pepper over high heat for 1 minute. Add shallots; stir-fry for 3 minutes or until well softened and beginning to brown. Add garlic; stir-fry for 1 minute. Add vinegar; cook, stirring, until it bubbles. Add tomatoes; cook, stirring often, for 1 minute or until glistening and hot to the touch.
3. Immediately scrape all the contents of the pan onto the lettuce. Toss until well combined. (You will notice a slight wilting of the lettuce.) Serve immediately with bread.

ARUGULA-BOCCONCINI SALAD

A modern cookbook is not complete without at least one recipe for arugula — a humble, smoky-nutty tasting weed that has gone from limited use in Italian kitchens to appear in virtually every menu worthy of the name. I remember it from my Istanbul days as *roka*, which was served on the side of grilled bonito tuna in the fall. I loved it then, and now have learned to love it on the side of just about anything. However you use it, be sure to dress it very simply, so as not to mask its memorable flavor.

2	bunches arugula	2
3 tbsp	extra virgin olive oil	45 mL
2 tbsp	red wine vinegar	25 mL
1/4 tsp	salt	1 mL
1/8 tsp	freshly ground black pepper	0.5 mL
8	bocconcini, halved (about 8 oz [250 g])	8

1. Wash and dry the arugula. Trim 1 inch (2.5 cm) off the stalk and discard, keeping the rest whole. Put in a salad bowl.

2. In a small bottle, shake together oil, vinegar, salt and pepper until slightly emulsified. Drizzle on the arugula; toss well to dress. Add bocconcini halves and fold to distribute, leaving some of them on top. Serve immediately.

GREEK BEAN AND TOMATO SALAD

Vine-ripened tomatoes, arguably the greatest gastronomic pleasure of summer, add the necessary sweetness to this substantial salad. It makes a wonderful lunch or starting course for a dinner, as well as a very useful addition to buffets since it lives nicely for a couple of hours after it's assembled. Feel free to use up to twice as much olive oil as called for in the recipe — that is, if calories aren't a problem — and you'll have a richer taste sensation.

2 cups	cooked white kidney beans *or* 1 can (19 oz [540 mL]), rinsed and drained	500 mL
2	ripe medium tomatoes, cut into 1/2-inch (1 cm) wedges	2
1/2 cup	thinly sliced red onions	125 mL
4	black olives, pitted and halved	4
	Few sprigs fresh parsley, chopped	
2 tbsp	red wine vinegar	25 mL
2 tbsp	extra virgin olive oil	25 mL
1/2 tsp	salt	2 mL
1/4 tsp	freshly ground black pepper	1 mL
4 oz	feta cheese in big crumbles	125 g
Half	red bell pepper, cut into thin strips	Half
1 tsp	olive oil	5 mL

1. Put beans into a bowl. Add tomatoes, red onions, olives and parsley. Do not toss.

2. In a small bowl, whisk together vinegar, 2 tbsp (25 mL) olive oil, salt and pepper until slightly emulsified. Sprinkle on beans; toss and fold until well mixed, but without mashing beans. Transfer the salad to a serving bowl. Distribute the feta crumbles decoratively on top.

3. In a small frying pan, heat 1 tsp (5 mL) oil over high heat; cook red pepper, turning often, for 3 to 4 minutes or until charred slightly and wilting. Decorate salad with the red peppers. Serve immediately, or cover and keep unrefrigerated for up to 2 hours.

ISTANBUL LEEKS

SERVES 4

This was one of my mother Despina's favorite "everyday" recipes. Perfect for a light lunch on its own, this savory dish works equally well as an accompaniment to meat or chicken for dinner. Istanbul gourmets eat these leeks (or *prassa*) at room temperature — as they do all their oil-cooked (versus butter-cooked) vegetables. Also, my mother, being an old-style Mediterranean, used at least twice as much oil as I (a more modern Med gourmet) suggest in this recipe. Vegetable oil is better than olive oil here, since it has a lighter taste. And, as always with leeks, care must be taken to wash out the grit that hides inside this flavorful vegetable.

1 lb	leeks (about 4 medium)	500 g
1/4 cup	vegetable oil	50 mL
1 tsp	sweet paprika	5 mL
1 tsp	salt	5 mL
1/2 tsp	freshly ground black pepper	2 mL
1/2 cup	short-grain rice	125 mL
8 oz	carrots (about 2), scraped and cut into 1/4-inch (5 mm) rounds	250 g
2 cups	boiling water	500 mL
1 tsp	granulated sugar	5 mL
2 tbsp	lemon juice	25 mL

1. To ensure that the leeks do not separate, make a 3-inch (7.5 cm) slit lengthwise through the middle of each leek. Wash sand away from central layers (where the white and green meet) through this slit. Cut off fibrous stem and discard. Slice the rest of the leek (green and white parts alike) into 1/2-inch (1 cm) chunks. Set aside.

2. In a pot heat oil with paprika, salt and pepper for 1 minute over medium-high heat, stirring. Add rice; stir-fry 2 minutes or until oily and sizzling. Add leeks and carrots; stir-fry 2 minutes or until everything is shiny and beginning to fry. Add water and sugar; stir to settle the ingredients, reduce heat to low and cover the pot tightly. Let cook for 35 to 40 minutes or until the vegetables and rice are all tender and much of the moisture has been absorbed.

3. Remove from heat and let stand alone, covered, for about 10 minutes. Uncover, sprinkle with lemon juice and stir gently. Serve immediately or let cool and serve at room temperature.

SUMMER ARTICHOKE SALAD

SERVES 4

Baby artichokes are a gift of nature. Here we find all the glory of grown-up artichokes, but with an edible choke (the fuzz that grows out and protects the heart) — which means zero work and all pleasure. Even more to the point, baby artichokes come to us already cooked (well, a bit overcooked) and ready to use. They're available bottled in oil or canned in water. If using ready-made, I recommend the canned. If using fresh, remove the outer leaves, cut 1/2 inch (1 cm) off the top, trim the stalk and boil over medium heat for 15 minutes until the hearts (bottoms) are easily pierced.

6	baby artichokes, cooked *or* 14-oz (398 mL) can artichoke hearts, rinsed and drained	6
Half	red bell pepper, cut into thin strips	Half
1/4 cup	thinly sliced red onions	50 mL
1	1-inch (2.5 cm) piece English cucumber, thinly sliced	1
5	black olives, pitted and halved	5
1	ripe large tomato, cut into 1/2-inch (1 cm) wedges	1
12	seedless grapes, halved	12
1 tsp	drained capers	5 mL
1	clove garlic, pressed	1
2 tbsp	extra virgin olive oil	25 mL
1 tbsp	white wine vinegar	15 mL
1 tbsp	lemon juice	15 mL
1/4 tsp	salt	1 mL
1/8 tsp	freshly ground black pepper	0.5 mL
	Few sprigs fresh parsley, chopped	

1. Cut the artichokes in half and put in a salad bowl. Add red pepper, onions, cucumber, olives, tomato, grapes and capers. Toss gently to mix.

2. In a small bowl, whisk together garlic, olive oil, vinegar, lemon juice, salt and pepper until slightly emulsified. Drizzle over the salad and toss gently to dress all the pieces, but without breaking up the artichokes too much. Garnish with parsley, and serve within 1 hour (cover if it has to wait, but do not refrigerate).

DANIAILE'S "LITTLE" CAULIFLOWER SALAD

SERVES 6

Cauliflower is a beautiful vegetable, although a puzzling one. Not quite tasty enough raw, it inevitably overcooks and tastes "off" if its florets are boiled whole. My great friend Daniaile Jarry found that if chopped into match-head-size bits and boiled quickly, cauliflower retains both flavor and texture. Here's a salad — dubbed "le petit choux-fleur de Daniaile" — that mixes these cauliflower bits with potatoes and aromatics.

1	head cauliflower	1
1 lb	potatoes, peeled and cut into 1/2-inch (1 cm) cubes (about 3 cups [750 mL])	500 g
1 cup	thinly sliced red onions	250 mL
Half	green pepper, very finely diced	Half
2 tbsp	drained capers	25 mL
2 tbsp	white wine vinegar	25 mL
1 tbsp	Dijon mustard	15 mL
1 tsp	salt	5 mL
1/2 tsp	freshly ground black pepper	2 mL
1/3 cup	fine olive oil	75 mL
	Several sprigs fresh parsley, chopped	

1. Separate florets of cauliflower from the large stalks. Reserve stalks for another use. Chop florets into tiny bits (match-head size). You should get about 4 cups (1 L). Set aside.

2. Boil potatoes in salted water on high heat for 5 to 6 minutes or until tender. Add reserved cauliflower bits and wait until water resumes boiling; from this point, boil for another 2 minutes or until the cauliflower is starting to become tender but is still crunchy. Drain immediately. Do not run cold water over the drained vegetables.

3. Transfer potatoes and cauliflower into a working bowl while still piping hot. Add onions, green pepper and capers. Toss gently a couple of times to mix.

4. In a small bowl, combine vinegar, mustard, salt and pepper. Add olive oil and whisk to combine. Pour sauce evenly over the vegetables. Toss gently but thoroughly to mix all the ingredients with the dressing.

5. If serving immediately (while still warm), transfer to a dish and garnish liberally with parsley. If for a buffet, the salad can wait up to 2 hours, covered and unrefrigerated. When ready to serve, mix to redistribute the dressing, transfer to a dish and garnish with parsley.

POTATO AND TUNA SALAD

In this recipe we take two all-time favorite picnic salads, rejuvenating both while creating a brand new salad in the process. The difference here is in the treatment of potato and tuna — both are presented in large chunks and mayo-free, thereby allowing us to enjoy texture as well as taste. If you wish, substitute the canned tuna with 8 oz (250 g) fresh tuna, grilled or sautéed and cut into 1/2-inch (1 cm) strips. Just make sure that you eat the salad soon after it's made — otherwise the cooked fresh tuna will turn fishy-tasting.

A number of complementary ingredients can be served alongside this salad for more festive occasions: hard-boiled halved eggs; wedges of fresh tomato; cucumber slices; olives; and even slices of your favorite fresh fruit.

1 lb	potatoes, scrubbed	500 g
2 tbsp	white wine vinegar	25 mL
1/2 tsp	salt	2 mL
1/4 tsp	freshly ground black pepper	1 mL
Half	green pepper, thinly sliced	Half
1 cup	thinly sliced red onions	250 mL
2	stalks celery, diced	2
1/4 cup	extra virgin olive oil	50 mL
1 tbsp	drained capers	15 mL
2	cans (each 6.5 oz [184 g]) chunk light tuna, drained	2
1 tsp	vegetable oil	5 mL
1/2 cup	whole pecans (about 2 oz [50 g])	125 mL
2 tbsp	extra virgin olive oil (optional)	25 mL
	Several sprigs fresh parsley, chopped	

1. Boil whole potatoes in salted water until easily pierceable, but before they start to crumble, about 30 minutes. Drain and cut while hot into 1/2-inch (1 cm) cubes. Transfer to a bowl; sprinkle evenly with vinegar, salt and pepper; toss gently to combine.

2. Add pepper slices, onions and celery; toss to combine. Add 1/4 cup (50 mL) olive oil and the capers; toss gently but thoroughly until combined. Add tuna; toss lightly to distribute the pieces but without mashing them at all. Transfer the tossed salad to a serving dish.

3. In a small frying pan, heat oil over high heat; add pecans and cook 2 to 3 minutes, turning them continuously to ensure they are browned but not burned. Decorate the salad with the fried pecans. If desired — that is, if calories are not a concern — drizzle 2 tbsp (25 mL) olive oil evenly over the salad.

4. Serve salad immediately or keep refrigerated for several hours. (Before serving, let it come to room temperature and toss it lightly so that it re-absorbs its dressing.) Garnish liberally with chopped parsley.

Moroccan Grapefruit Olive Salad

Here's a dish that does great service as a light opening course and admirably on the side of things like couscous, paella or lasagna. The success of this delicious, very "adult" salad depends on its appearance which, in turn, depends on whether you're able to peel and skin the grapefruit segments while keeping them intact. Oranges can substitute for grapefruit — although they're even more tedious to prepare. Using ready-skinned segments is always an option.

2	grapefruits	2
1/2 cup	thinly sliced red onions	125 mL
8	black olives, pitted and chopped in slivers	8
3 tbsp	extra virgin olive oil	45 mL
1 tbsp	white wine vinegar	15 mL
1 tsp	lemon juice	5 mL
1/2 tsp	sweet paprika	2 mL
1/2 tsp	salt	2 mL
1/4 tsp	freshly ground black pepper	1 mL
1	clove garlic, pressed	1
4	whole leaves lettuce	4
	Few sprigs fresh coriander or parsley, chopped	

1. With a sharp knife, cut peel and pith away from whole grapefruits; cut on either side of membranes to release grapefruit segments. Put skinned grapefruit segments into a salad bowl. Scatter onions and olives over the grapefruit. Do not mix.

2. In a small bowl, whisk together the olive oil, vinegar, lemon juice, paprika, salt, pepper and garlic until slightly emulsified. Drizzle dressing over the grapefruit, onions and olives in the salad bowl. Fold gently, several times to mix ingredients and distribute the dressing. The salad can wait, covered and unrefrigerated, for up to 1 hour.

3. Place a lettuce leaf on each of 4 plates. Portion out the salad equally on top of the lettuce. Garnish with coriander and serve immediately.

Jane's Chicken Salad

Of many wonderful visits to London, overnights with Jane and Michael Sutherland are especially memorable. Excellent people and food-buffs to boot — an unbeatable combination, when it comes to friends. Jane, a caterer of considerable reputation, invented this sunny salad, elegant with its long strips of chicken and roasted hazelnuts.

A note about mayonnaise: If store-bought mayonnaise is not good enough (and it never is), you can make your own: Whisk 1 egg yolk; add 1 tbsp (15 mL) white wine vinegar and 1 tsp (5 mL) Dijon mustard; whisk again. Add up to 1 cup (250 mL) olive oil in drops at first and then in a thin stream, all the while whisking vigorously. Season to taste with salt and pepper. Keep refrigerated and use within 48 hours.

To roast raw hazelnuts: Bake in a 350° F (180° C) oven for 15 minutes. Let cool, and rub them between your hands. Most of the skins will fall off, leaving behind the browned nuts.

2 tbsp	lemon juice	25 mL
Half	green apple, thinly sliced	Half
1	stalk celery, chopped	1
1/2 cup	thinly sliced red onions	125 mL
20	red seedless grapes, halved	20
1	small tomato, cut into 1/2-inch (1 cm) cubes, with juices	1
	Few sprigs fresh tarragon and/or parsley, chopped	
1 tbsp	olive oil	15 mL
8 oz	boneless skinless chicken breasts	250 g
1/2 to 1 cup	mayonnaise	125 to 250 mL
	Salt and pepper to taste	
2 oz	roasted skinned hazelnuts (about 1/3 cup [75 mL])	50 g

1. Put 1 tbsp (15 mL) of the lemon juice in a bowl. Add green apple slices and roll in the lemon juice to coat. Add celery, red onions, grapes, tomato and most of the chopped herbs. Fold the ingredients together until well mixed.

2. In a frying pan, heat olive oil over high heat for 1 minute. Add chicken breasts; sear 1 to 2 minutes per side or until browned. Reduce heat to medium-high and continue cooking for 4 minutes per side or until cooked through (cut into the chicken to make sure). Transfer the chicken to a cutting board to cool. With pan still on the heat, add remaining lemon juice. Deglaze the pan, scraping up any brown bits; let it sizzle for 30 seconds. With a spatula, scrape sauce onto the vegetable-fruit mixture.

3. With a sharp knife, slice the cooled chicken into long 1/4-inch (5 mm) strips. Add chicken strips to the bowl. Fold a couple of times to mix in, without damaging chicken strips too much. Add mayonnaise and salt and pepper to taste; fold gently to mix. Transfer salad to a serving dish and garnish with the remaining herbs and the hazelnuts. Serve immediately.

ITALIAN SQUID SALAD

SERVES 4

Call it squid or calamari, this nutritious, relatively lean seafood becomes a delicacy in the hands of the Italians. Whether grilled (see recipe, page 88) or poached (as in this recipe), squid is all about texture — a tender crunchiness that is achieved with undercooking. Its subtle taste is a perfect complement to the various sunshine flavors that are brought together in this uplifting start to any main course.

If you prefer a salad with more variety, try a half-and-half combination of squid and shell-on medium shrimp instead of squid alone; cook both seafoods at the same time as described in Step 1, then peel the cooked shrimp; proceed with the recipe, keeping shrimp and squid together.

1 lb	cleaned squid	500 g
3 cups	water	750 mL
Half	lemon, cut in quarters	Half
1	bay leaf	1
1/2 tsp	dried basil	2 mL
2 tbsp	lemon juice	25 mL
1 tbsp	balsamic vinegar	15 mL
	Salt and pepper to taste	
1/4 cup	extra virgin olive oil	50 mL
1/2 cup	thinly sliced red onions	125 mL
Half	green pepper, thinly sliced	Half
1 tbsp	drained capers	15 mL
1	medium tomato, cut into 1/2-inch (1 cm) cubes	1
4	large lettuce leaves	4
	Few sprigs chopped fresh basil and/or parsley	

1. Slice squid bodies into 1/2-inch (1 cm) rings. Cut tentacles at their base to halve them. Rinse and set aside. In a saucepan bring water to a boil; stir in lemon, bay leaf and basil; boil 2 minutes. Reduce heat to medium and add squid; cook 5 minutes for *al dente* texture or 8 to 9 minutes if you like squid more tender. Drain, discarding liquid, lemon pieces and bay leaf. Transfer squid to a bowl.

2. Immediately add lemon juice, vinegar, salt and pepper; toss well to coat. Add olive oil, and toss again. Add onions, green pepper and capers; toss to combine. (If time permits, this salad improves if allowed to rest as is, covered and unrefrigerated for 30 minutes to 1 hour.)

3. Add tomato cubes and any tomato juices that have accumulated and toss to combine. Line 4 plates with lettuce leaves and distribute the salad evenly among them, including the dressing. Top with a liberal garnish of herbs and serve.

SMOKED SALMON AND AVOCADO SALAD

SERVES 3 OR 4

Smoked salmon, a decidedly Northern treat, appears to have arrived in sunnier climes. These days you can find it everywhere, from Athens to Malaga. Here we combine it with avocado — another newcomer to the Mediterranean — for a taste combination that knows no borders. This salad of pastel colors and summery tastes will please even the most demanding dinner guests. The only caveats are that you use a ripe, unblemished avocado and a really good (which, sad to say, means expensive) smoked salmon.

2 tbsp	lemon juice	25 mL
1	ripe avocado	1
1/4 cup	finely minced red onions	50 mL
1 tbsp	extra virgin olive oil	15 mL
1 tsp	drained capers	5 mL
Pinch	salt	Pinch
4 oz	sliced smoked salmon	125 g
	Freshly ground black pepper, to taste	
1	2-inch (5 cm) piece English cucumber, thinly sliced	1
1	medium tomato, cut into 1/2-inch (1 cm) cubes	1
	Several sprigs fresh coriander and/or parsley, chopped	

1. Put lemon juice into a bowl. Peel and slice (or scoop) avocado into bite-size pieces. Fold into the lemon juice to avoid discoloration. Add red onions, olive oil, capers and salt. Fold all ingredients together carefully until just mixed, taking care not to mash the avocado.

2. Cut the smoked salmon slices into strips 1/2 inch (1 cm) wide. Scatter the pieces onto the avocado. Sprinkle with black pepper. Fold the salmon into the salad carefully.

3. Arrange cucumber slices on the bottom of a serving plate. Heap the salmon-avocado salad onto the middle of the cucumbers, leaving a border of cucumber visible. Garnish with the cubes of tomato and chopped herbs. Serve within 20 minutes.

MARINATED SALMON WITH RED ONION AND CRÈME FRAÎCHE

SERVES 3 OR 4

Marinated salmon has become increasingly popular, particularly the Scandinavian gravlax. Here is an Italian-style recipe that cures the fish with lemon juice — which, happily, also cuts the waiting period down from gravlax's 2 to 3 days to a mere 2 or 3 hours.

Mind you, it involves the admittedly unpleasant task of slicing raw salmon and (especially) removing the needle bones that run down the fat part of the fillet from the head halfway to the tail. (They're best pulled by thin pliers or, even better, by the fishmonger, if you ask nicely.) The crème-fraîche can be faked at home by using 1 cup (250 mL) sour cream, mixing in 1 tbsp (15 mL) lemon juice and enriching it by mixing in 2 tbsp (25 mL) whipping (35%) cream.

10-inch (25 cm) ceramic or glass pie plate

1/4 cup	extra virgin olive oil	50 mL
1/4 cup	lemon juice	50 mL
12 oz to 1 lb	fillet of fresh salmon, deboned with skin left on	375 to 500 g
	Salt and pepper to taste	
1 cup	thinly sliced red onions	250 mL
1 tbsp	drained capers	15 mL
	Few sprigs fresh parsley, chopped	
1 cup	crème fraîche	250 mL

1. Put 1 tbsp (15 mL) each oil and lemon juice on the bottom of pie plate and spread to cover the bottom and sides. Take salmon (preferably cold, straight from the refrigerator) and, running your fingers on the surface, make sure all bones are out. Wipe surface of the salmon. Using a very sharp knife, cut the salmon towards the thin end in slices 1/4 inch (5 mm) thick — even slightly thinner if you can. The knife will stop on the skin; remove slice from the skin by sliding knife forward. Lay slice on oil-lemon mixture in the pie plate. Continue slicing until you've covered the whole surface of the plate.

2. Sprinkle salmon slices with salt and pepper. Scatter some of the red onions, capers and parsley on top. Drizzle evenly with another 1 tbsp (15 mL) each of lemon and oil.

3. Repeat procedure to make another 2 layers, using all ingredients. (If salmon slices are not thin enough you may only get 1 more layer.) Cover pie plate tightly with plastic wrap and refrigerate for at least 2 hours or up to 24 hours. (For best results, refrigerate 4 to 5 hours.)

Recipe continues...

AROMATIC FISH SOUP (PAGE 70) ➤
OVERLEAF: SUMMER ARTICHOKE SALAD (PAGE 55)

4. Take salmon out of the fridge and let it warm to room temperature, about 30 minutes. Carefully pick up salmon slices and distribute among 4 plates. Spoon onions, capers and parsley onto the salmon; moisten each plate with 1 tsp (5 mL) of the marinating juice (discard any leftover juice). Serve with a dollop of crème fraîche in the middle of each portion, and the rest of the crème on the side.

◄ FILET OF SOLE WITH CORIANDER PESTO (PAGE 84)

MIXED PEPPERS AND SEAFOOD SALAD

Ever since they were "discovered" by North Americans in the 1970s, cooked bell peppers have been tremendously popular — not only for their sweet, flavorful flesh, but also for their remarkable versatility as an accompaniment to virtually any dish (something the Italians have known for millennia). As a result, our markets are now full of peppers of all colors, including the usual green and red, as well as yellow, orange — even purple. Here's a recipe for whatever color peppers you want to combine with a zesty flash-fry of seafood and, for good measure, some aromatic vegetables.

1/4 cup	olive oil	50 mL
1/2 tsp	salt	2 mL
1/4 tsp	freshly ground black pepper	1 mL
4	bell peppers, different colors, cut lengthwise into 8 wedges	4
8 oz	bay scallops	250 g
1/4 cup	all-purpose flour	50 mL
8 oz	raw medium shrimps, shelled and deveined	250 g
1 tbsp	finely chopped garlic	15 mL
1 tsp	dried basil	5 mL
2 tbsp	balsamic vinegar	25 mL
2 tbsp	white wine *or* water	25 mL
2 tbsp	thinly sliced red onions	25 mL
1 tbsp	drained capers	15 mL
1 tbsp	extra virgin olive oil	15 mL
	Several sprigs fresh basil or parsley, chopped	

1. In a large nonstick frying pan, heat 2 tbsp (25 mL) of the olive oil, salt and pepper over medium-high heat for 30 seconds. Add peppers and cook, turning often, 8 to 10 minutes or until the peppers are soft and the skin has begun to char. Transfer peppers to a platter; arrange attractively in alternating colors having some skin-side up and some flesh-side up. Set aside the frying pan without wiping.

2. Dredge the scallops in flour and toss in a wire strainer to shake off excess. Return frying pan to high heat. Add remaining olive oil, salt and pepper; heat for 30 seconds. Add scallops and shrimp; actively sauté, turning often, for 1 minute or until the scallops are lightly browning and the shrimps are turning pink. Immediately add garlic and basil; cook, stirring actively, for 1 minute. Add 1 tbsp (15 mL) of the balsamic vinegar; cook, stirring, for 30 seconds. Add white wine; cook, stirring, for 30 seconds or until bubbling.

3. Pour seafood and all its sauce evenly over the peppers. Scatter red onions and capers over the salad. In a small bottle, shake together remaining balsamic vinegar with olive oil until slightly emulsified; drizzle evenly over the salad. Garnish with chopped basil and serve immediately while still warm.

LOBSTER SALAD

Lobster is a wonderfully troublesome food. Yes, it's expensive, as well as messy and difficult (not to mention dangerous) to handle. But few things impress important dinner guests as much as the prospect of that succulent flesh melting in their mouths. Here's an Istanbul recipe with which my mother, Despina, certainly impressed those of her guests lucky enough to get it. The recipe allows for all the messy stuff (cooking the beasts, shelling them, etc.) to happen in advance. You can, if you wish, buy pre-cooked lobster (but please, only from reputable fishmongers) — preferably in the shell. If using shelled lobster meat, use 8 to 12 oz (250 to 375 g).

2 1/2 to 3 lbs	lobsters	1.25 to 1.5 kg
1/2 cup	thinly sliced red onions	125 mL
2	green onions, chopped	2
2 tbsp	lemon juice	25 mL
	Salt and pepper to taste	
3 tbsp	extra virgin olive oil	45 mL
1 tbsp	drained capers	15 mL
1	medium tomato, cut into 1/2-inch (1 cm) wedges	1
	Several sprigs fresh parsley, chopped	
	Lemon wedges	

1. Boil lobsters for 10 to 12 minutes in salted water. Rinse and refresh them in cold running water. When cool enough to handle, shell them. Cut the meat in 1-inch (2.5 cm) chunks and put in a working bowl.

2. Add onions, green onions, lemon juice, and salt and pepper to taste. Mix gently but thoroughly to coat. Add olive oil and capers; mix gently but thoroughly once more. Transfer to a serving dish and let marinate, covered and unrefrigerated, for about 15 minutes. (If making in advance, the recipe can be prepared to this point, then kept covered and refrigerated for several hours; let lobster warm to room temperature for 30 minutes and stir before continuing.)

3. Arrange tomato wedges decoratively on the salad. Serve garnished with parsley and lemon wedges.

FISH AND SEAFOOD

Aromatic Fish Soup   70

Fish with Peppers and Olives   72

Broiled Halibut with Black Butter   73

Broiled Salmon with Green Tapenade and
Endive   74

Crusted Salmon with Green Peppercorn
Sauce   76

Swordfish with Balsamic Vinegar   78

Swordfish Kebabs with Parsley Sauce   79

Red Snapper Barcelona   80

Flash-Fried Red Snapper with Green
Onions   82

Spanish Shrimp with Paprika   83

Filet of Sole with Coriander Pesto   84

Shrimp with Tomato and Feta   86

Garlic Shrimp with Mushrooms   87

Calamari, Two Ways   88

Calamari Fricassee   90

Broiled Scallops on Eggplant Purée   92

Sautéed Scallops in Wine-Lemon Sauce   94

AROMATIC FISH SOUP

Fish soup is as much a part of life in the fish-rich Mediterranean as fishing itself. Every country has its own version, but the French claim the honor of the "state of the art," with their justly famous bouillabaisse. It is impossible for us to recreate any of the originals accurately, because we simply don't have the appropriate fish. But by using the right combination of aromatic vegetables, herbs and garlic — and by adding from our own available fish and seafood — we have come up with this delicious and utterly accessible version of a meal-size fish soup.

Fresh salmon heads are available cheaply at all fish-mongers.

1/4 cup	olive oil	50 mL
1/2 tsp	salt	2 mL
1/2 tsp	freshly ground black pepper	2 mL
2 cups	roughly chopped onions	500 mL
4	stalks celery with leaves, cut into 1-inch (2.5 cm) pieces	4
1/2 tsp	fennel seeds	2 mL
2 lbs	plum tomatoes, diced *or* 1 can (28 oz [796 mL]) plum tomatoes	1 kg
10	cloves garlic, thinly sliced	10
2	bay leaves	2
1/2 tsp	dried basil	2 mL
1/2 tsp	dried oregano	2 mL
6 cups	water	1.5 L
	Few sprigs fresh parsley	
2 1/2 lbs	fish heads (about 2 salmon heads)	1.25 kg
2 cups	peeled cubed potatoes	500 mL
1 1/2 lbs	skinless boneless fillet of salmon, cod, halibut (or combination) cut into 1/2-inch (1 cm) cubes	750 g
8 oz	medium shrimp (optional), shelled and deveined	250 g
1 tbsp	lemon juice	15 mL
	Salt and pepper to taste	
4	large thick slices French bread, toasted	4
	Few chervil or celery leaves, chopped	

1. In a large saucepan over high heat, combine olive oil, salt and pepper. Add onions, celery and fennel seeds. Sauté, stirring frequently, for 5 minutes or until beginning to brown. Immediately add tomatoes, garlic, bay leaves, oregano and basil; cook, stirring, for 5 to 6 minutes or until sauce-like.

2. Stir in water; bring to boil. Add parsley and fish heads. Reduce heat to medium-high and cook for 35 to 40 minutes on a steady bubbling (but not rolling) boil, stirring infrequently.

3. Take off heat. Cover and let cool 1 to 2 hours to develop flavors. Strain, pushing down on ingredients and mashed down pulp to extract all the broth. Discard leftovers from strainer. (Recipe can be prepared to this point up to 2 days in advance; cover and refrigerate broth.)

4. Bring the strained broth to a boil. Add potatoes, reduce heat to medium-high and cook for 10 to 15 minutes or until soft and pierceable. Add fish and shrimp (if using); reduce heat to medium and cook 3 to 4 minutes or until the fish is tender but not overcooked. Stir in lemon juice. Season to taste with salt and pepper.

5. Place a toasted slice of bread into each of 4 bowls. Top each with one-quarter of the soup, making sure that potatoes and fish are distributed evenly. Garnish generously with chopped chervil and serve immediately.

FISH WITH PEPPERS AND OLIVES

SERVES 4

Fillets of lean, white fish like cod, turbot, halibut and the expensive red snapper and sea bass are wonderfully easy and particularly tender and flaky if quick-poached in a complex sauce that is bursting with "southern" flavors. The only warning is to avoid overcooking the fish. Even the 6 to 7 minutes of Step 2, might be too long by 1 to 2 minutes if your fillets are thinner than 1 inch (2.5 cm).

1/4 cup	olive oil	50 mL
1/2 tsp	salt	2 mL
1/4 tsp	freshly ground black pepper	1 mL
Half	green pepper, cut into 1/2-inch (1 cm) squares	Half
Half	red bell pepper, cut into 1/2-inch (1 cm) squares	Half
1 tbsp	chopped garlic	15 mL
1 tbsp	lemon zest, cut into ribbons	15 mL
2 cups	diced peeled tomatoes, with juices (about 12 oz [375 g]) *or* canned tomatoes	500 mL
1 tbsp	lemon juice	15 mL
1 tsp	drained capers	5 mL
10	black olives, pitted and halved	10
4	pieces each 5 oz (150 g) boneless, skinless fillets of cod, halibut or turbot	4
	Steamed rice as an accompaniment	
	Few sprigs fresh basil or parsley, chopped	

1. In a large frying pan, heat olive oil, salt and pepper over high heat for 1 minute. Add green and red pepper squares; stir-fry for 1 to 2 minutes or until their skin begins to char. Add garlic and lemon zest; stir-fry for 1 minute until the garlic is browning. Add tomatoes, lemon juice and capers; cook 2 to 3 minutes or until the tomatoes begin to break up and a sauce is forming. Add olives and stir-fry for 1 minute. (The recipe can wait at this point; to continue, bring the sauce back to boiling.)

2. Reduce heat to medium. Add fish pieces and fit into the sauce, spooning some sauce and vegetables over the fish as well as all around it. Cover and let cook for 6 to 7 minutes or until firm to the touch. Take off heat. Let rest, covered, for 5 minutes.

3. Arrange alongside steamed rice, generously spooning vegetables and sauce over the fish and the rice. Garnish with chopped basil and serve immediately.

BROILED HALIBUT WITH BLACK BUTTER

Charlotte Dix, my wonderful friend and frequent collaborator, turned me on to black butter and my waistline has never recovered. It means eating a significant amount of butter, but it makes any white-fleshed fish, whether grilled or poached, such a pleasure, that... well, what's the point of worrying? Originally invented for poached skate wings, I present it here for halibut (a more accessible fish) which I broil to save myself the chores of poaching. Something red — a cherry tomato, a strip of red pepper — and a small boiled potato is all you'll need on the side.

Baking sheet
Preheat broiler

2	halibut steaks (about 1 lb [500 g]), 3/4-inch (2 cm) thick	2
1 tsp	butter	5 mL
1/4 cup	salted butter	50 mL
1/8 tsp	salt	0.5 mL
1/8 tsp	freshly ground black pepper	0.5 mL
1 tsp	black or white sesame seeds	5 mL
1 tbsp	balsamic vinegar	15 mL
	Few sprigs fresh parsley, chopped	

1. Rub 1 tsp (5 mL) butter on both sides of the halibut steaks. Put them on a baking sheet. Broil for 4 to 5 minutes each side or until cooked through.

2. Meanwhile, in a small pot, combine 1/4 cup (50 mL) butter, salt and pepper. Cook over medium-high heat, stirring, for about 8 minutes or until browned. (It'll foam during the last 2 minutes, so you have to watch and stir actively to make sure it isn't burning; despite its name, *beurre noir* is ruined if it turns black.) Remove from heat. Add sesame seeds and vinegar in quick succession (careful, it'll splutter). Set aside.

3. Put halibut steaks in the centers of 2 warm plates. Pour portions of black butter (including its solids) over, allowing it to pool around the fish. Garnish with chopped parsley and serve immediately.

BROILED SALMON WITH GREEN TAPENADE AND ENDIVE

SERVES 4

A tapenade made with green olives is sweeter than its black-olive counterpart — and it works as wonderfully with fish as the black variety works with meat and chicken. Here it's combined with dill and onion to partner salmon and grilled endive. The green olives I recommend are the large, meaty variety of which the indicated quantity (8) should be enough. The much milder, supermarket variety are generally smaller and you'll need twice as many (16).

Baking sheet
Preheat broiler

8 to 16	green olives, pitted and chopped (about 1/3 cup [75 mL])	8 to 16
1/4 cup	chopped packed fresh dill	50 mL
1/4 cup	grated onions, with juices	50 mL
1 tbsp	pine nuts	15 mL
2 tbsp	lemon juice	25 mL
2 tbsp	extra virgin olive oil	25 mL
1/4 tsp	freshly ground black pepper	1 mL
1 tbsp	extra virgin olive oil	15 mL
1	Belgian endive, sliced lengthwise into 1/4-inch (5 mm) strips	1
1 1/2 lbs	skinless boneless salmon fillet, cut into in 4 equal pieces	750 g
	Few sprigs fresh dill	
	Few thin strips red bell pepper	
	Steamed rice or freshly boiled potatoes as an accompaniment	

1. In a food processor combine olives, dill, onions, pine nuts, lemon juice, 2 tbsp (25 mL) olive oil and black pepper. Process, scraping down sides of bowl once, for 1 minute or until coarse but well blended. You should have 1/2 cup (125 mL) green tapenade.

2. Smear 1 tbsp (15 mL) olive oil on baking sheet. Add endive strips and turn them in the oil until thoroughly coated. Push the endive to the sides. Place salmon pieces in the vacated middle. Spread 1 tbsp (15 mL) tapenade thinly on each piece of salmon to cover top surface.

3. On the middle rack of the oven, broil (without turning) 8 to 10 minutes if fillets are from the tail end (which is thinner) and 10 to 12 minutes if they are from the head end. (The minimum times will leave a moist center; the maximum times will give you fish that is well-cooked right through.)

4. Distribute the endive strips (which should be wilted and somewhat charred) in the center of 4 warmed plates. Place the salmon pieces on the beds of endive. Add 1 tbsp (15 mL) fresh tapenade on the center of each nugget and garnish with sprigs of dill and criss-crossed strips of red pepper. Serve immediately, accompanied by rice or freshly boiled potatoes.

CRUSTED SALMON WITH GREEN PEPPERCORN SAUCE

SERVES 4

In the old days, we used to think that peppercorns came only in one shade — black (as in "black pepper"). Now that our gastronomic horizons have been broadened to include delicacies from all continents, peppercorns of other colors have joined our lexicon of spices. The most distinctive of these are the green peppercorns of Madagascar — soft and full of exotic taste, packed in brine. They don't quite go with everything (as black pepper does), but they do marvellous things to mushrooms and goat cheese (see recipe, page 30), and elevate this simply crusted salmon into haute cuisine. (Leftover green peppercorns can be stored indefinitely in their brine, covered, in the fridge.)

1/2 cup	yellow cornmeal	125 mL
1 tbsp	sweet paprika	15 mL
1 1/2 lbs	skinless boneless salmon fillet, cut into 4 equal pieces	750 g
1/2 cup	milk	125 mL
3 tbsp	olive oil	45 mL
2 tbsp	lemon juice	25 mL
1 tbsp	drained green peppercorns	15 mL
1 cup	fish stock *or* white wine	250 mL
1 tbsp	softened butter	15 mL
	Few sprigs fresh parsley, chopped	
	Freshly boiled potatoes as an accompaniment	

1. On a plate stir together cornmeal and paprika until more-or-less combined. Dunk salmon into milk and then roll all sides in the cornmeal to dredge well. Set aside. (You can discard leftover cornmeal and milk.)

2. In a large nonstick pan, heat olive oil over high heat for 1 minute or until just about to smoke. Add dredged salmon and reduce heat to medium-high. Fry the salmon for 3 to 4 minutes on each side or until fish is crusted and browned all over and is slightly firm to the touch. (The success of this dish depends on the proper execution of this step; exact timing will depend on the thickness of the salmon — whether from the thinner tail end or the thicker head end, as well as how well you like it done. If you must have it well done, then fry over a lower [medium] heat for 5 to 6 minutes each side, so that the fish cooks through before the cornmeal burns.)

3. Remove the fish to a plate and cover to keep warm. Return the pan with its leftover oil to high heat. Immediately add lemon juice and green peppercorns; cook, stirring, for 1 minute until sizzling and starting to color. Add fish stock; cook, stirring, for 3 minutes or until bubbling actively and reduced by at least a third. Remove from heat. Stir in butter until it melts and slightly thickens the sauce.

4. Put pools of the sauce (with the peppercorns) on 4 warmed plates. Place the salmon in the middle of the pools. Accompany with a fresh boiled potato, garnish with chopped parsley and serve immediately.

SWORDFISH WITH BALSAMIC VINEGAR

SERVES 2

Swordfish is a meaty, firm-fleshed fish that ends up miraculously tender if undercooked, and is sturdy enough to be handled with no intimidation whatsoever. It can be fried or grilled, or it can be cut into cubes and skewered (as in SWORDFISH KEBABS WITH PARSLEY SAUCE; see recipe, facing page). The only drawback is that swordfish, when fresh (as is desirable), is often very expensive. The frozen variety is substantially cheaper, but expect a 25% loss of quality in texture, tenderness and flavor. Here's a recipe for swordfish steak with a sauce from Toronto superchef Leo Schipani. It combines a number of high-voltage flavor ingredients without overwhelming the original taste of the fish.

Preheat grill or broiler

1 lb	swordfish steak, 3/4-inch (2 cm) thick, cut into 2 pieces	500 g
1 tbsp	olive oil	15 mL
1	bay leaf, crumbled	1
1 tbsp	balsamic vinegar	15 mL
2 tbsp	extra virgin olive oil	25 mL
1/8 tsp	salt	0.5 mL
1/8 tsp	freshly ground black pepper	0.5 mL
2	softened sun-dried tomatoes, cut into quarters	2
4	black olives, pitted and chopped into small bits	4
2 tbsp	finely minced red onions	25 mL
	Few sprigs fresh parsley, chopped	

1. Wash and wipe swordfish steaks. Brush both sides with 1 tbsp (15 mL) olive oil. Sprinkle bay leaf crumbles over top sides of the fish. Grill or broil the fish with the bay leaf side facing up for 3 to 5 minutes. Turn over and cook second side for 2 to 4 minutes. (Cook the maximum times if you prefer medium-well done; the shorter times will leave a pink middle.)

2. Meanwhile prepare the sauce: In a bowl whisk together vinegar, olive oil, salt and pepper until emulsified, about 1 minute. Stir in sun-dried tomatoes, olives and red onions.

3. When the fish is ready, transfer each steak to a warm plate. Pick off leftover bay leaf pieces. Heap half the sauce on the middle of each steak. Sprinkle chopped parsley over the whole plate and serve immediately.

SWORDFISH KEBABS WITH PARSLEY SAUCE

SERVES 4

There were many kebabs (grills) in my Mediterranean childhood, but the most succulently deluxe of all was (and still is) the festively skewered-grilled swordfish featured in this recipe. Deluxe, because swordfish has always been (and very much still is) expensive, and therefore a rare delicacy; and succulent because this already-tender, juicy item ends up twice as much so when grilled between peppers and onions. Swordfish is at its best when grilled on a barbecue. It can be broiled in an oven, but only in a pinch.

Eight 8-inch (20 cm) metal skewers
***or* wooden skewers soaked in water**
Preheat grill or broiler

3 tbsp	extra virgin olive oil	45 mL
2 tbsp	finely chopped fresh parsley	25 mL
1 tbsp	lemon juice	15 mL
1 tsp	balsamic vinegar	5 mL
1/4 tsp	salt	1 mL
1/8 tsp	freshly ground black pepper	0.5 mL
1 1/2 lbs	boneless skinless swordfish, cut into 1-inch (2.5 cm) cubes	750 g
Half	red bell pepper, cut into 1-inch (2.5 cm) squares	Half
Half	green or yellow pepper, cut into 1-inch (2.5 cm) squares	Half
1	onion, cut into 1-inch (2.5 cm) chunks	1
1 tsp	olive oil	5 mL
2	bay leaves, crumbled	2
	Tomato wedges	
	Freshly boiled potatoes or steamed rice as an accompaniment	

1. Make the parsley sauce: In a small bowl, whisk together 3 tbsp (45 mL) olive oil, parsley, lemon juice, vinegar, salt and pepper. Set aside.

2. Skewer swordfish, alternating it with pieces of red pepper, green pepper and onion. Brush the skewers with a little oil and scatter crumbled bay leaves over everything.

3. Grill or broil the skewers for 3 to 5 minutes; turn over and cook 2 to 4 minutes. (Cook the maximum times if you prefer medium-well done; the shorter times will leave a pink middle.)

4. Garnish with wedges of tomato, accompany with a potato or rice and serve immediately with parsley sauce on the side for spooning at table.

RED SNAPPER BARCELONA

Here we present fillets of red snapper, smothered with a very Hispanic mantle of peppers, onions and tomato. The idea for this dish might have started in Barcelona (where I first sampled it), but it reached its zenith in Vera Cruz, Mexico, where they call it *huachinango Veracruzana*, and serve it with lime and coriander (instead of lemon and parsley), and a kick-ass hot sauce on the side. It's a lovely dish, as long as you stick with the relatively easy task of making only 2 portions at a time.

1 tbsp	olive oil	15 mL
1/4 tsp	salt	1 mL
1/4 tsp	freshly ground black pepper	1 mL
1/2 cup	thinly sliced onions	125 mL
1/4 cup	thinly sliced red bell peppers	50 mL
1/4 cup	thinly sliced green peppers	50 mL
1 tbsp	finely chopped garlic	15 mL
1 tbsp	lemon zest, cut into ribbons	15 mL
2 tbsp	lemon juice	25 mL
1	large tomato, cut into 1/2-inch (1 cm) wedges	1
1/2 tsp	dried thyme	2 mL
2	fillets fresh red snapper, boned, skin on (about 12 oz [375 g] from a whole fish of 1 1/2 lb [750 g])	2
1/4 cup	all-purpose flour	50 mL
2 tbsp	olive oil	25 mL
	Few sprigs fresh parsley, chopped	
	Lemon wedges	
	Steamed rice as an accompaniment	

1. In a nonstick frying pan, heat 1 tbsp (15 mL) olive oil, salt and pepper over high heat for 30 seconds. Add onions and peppers; stir-fry for 2 minutes or until wilted and beginning to char. Add garlic and lemon zest; stir-fry for 30 seconds. Add lemon juice; cook, stirring, for 30 seconds or until sizzling and browning. Add tomato and thyme; stir-fry for 2 minutes or until the tomatoes are threatening to break up. Remove from heat and set aside in the pan.

2. Lightly dredge snapper fillets in flour. Set aside.

3. In a large nonstick frying pan, heat 2 tbsp (25 mL) olive oil over high heat for 1 minute. Add fillets, skin-side down; fry for 4 minutes to brown. (The fillets will bunch up when they first hit the oil; don't worry, this is normal.) Turn over carefully; cook for 2 minutes or until lightly brown. Arrange cooked fillets flesh-side up on 2 warmed plates; cover to keep warm.

4. Return the pan with the sauce to high heat; cook, stirring, for just under 1 minute until warmed through. Heap equal amounts of sauce and vegetables on each fillet. Garnish with chopped parsley and a wedge of lemon. Accompany with plain rice and serve immediately.

FLASH-FRIED RED SNAPPER WITH GREEN ONIONS

SERVES 2 °

With its delicate, snow-white flesh, red snapper is justly a favorite of fish lovers. Of course, as is always true of good things, it's on the pricey side. So here's a special treat for you and a loved one — a small feast for two that is easy to make, and would cost a fortune in a restaurant. The recipe can be multiplied, but beware: aside from the cost, additional portions will require cooking in several batches, or necessitate juggling multiple frying pans, with the attendant risk of a mishap.

2	fillets fresh red snapper, boned, skin on (about 12 oz [375 g] from a whole fish of 1 1/2 lb [750 g])	2
1/4 cup	all-purpose flour	50 mL
2 tbsp	olive oil	25 mL
1/4 tsp	salt	1 mL
1/4 tsp	freshly ground black pepper	1 mL
1 tsp	crumbled dried rosemary	5 mL
1 tbsp	lemon juice	15 mL
1/2 cup	fish stock *or* white wine	125 mL
1/2 cup	chopped green onions	125 mL
1 tbsp	softened butter	15 mL
	Boiled potatoes as an accompaniment	

1. Lightly dredge red snapper fillets in flour. Set aside.
2. In a large nonstick frying pan, heat olive oil, salt and pepper over high heat for 1 minute. Add fillets, skin-side down; fry 4 minutes to brown. (The fillets will bunch up when they first hit the oil; don't worry, this is normal.) Turn over carefully; cook for 2 minutes or until lightly brown. Arrange cooked fillets flesh-side up on 2 warmed plates; cover to keep warm.
3. Return the pan with any leftover oil to medium-high heat. Add rosemary; stir-fry for 15 seconds. Add lemon juice; cook, stirring, for 30 seconds or until sizzling and starting to brown. Add fish stock; cook, stirring, for 2 to 3 minutes or until bubbling actively and reduced by a third. Add most of the green onions; cook for 1 minute or until onions are lighter in color and wilted. Remove from heat and stir in the butter until it melts and slightly thickens the sauce.
4. Pour equal portions of the sauce and cooked green onions on each fillet. Garnish with remaining (uncooked) green onions, accompany with a boiled potato and serve immediately.

SPANISH SHRIMP WITH PAPRIKA

SERVES 2 AS A MAIN COURSE OR 4 AS A STARTER

A favorite snack at Spanish tapas bars, these shrimp make for a hands-on, messy but entertaining nosh, either for a starting course, or as a main course alongside rice and salad. The shells (minus the legs) are left on for a reason: the shrimp end up more succulent, so you're free to enjoy them just as they are once shelled at table or, more richly, by dipping them in their cooking sauce — a lusty concoction of oil, garlic and spices. A good supply of paper napkins is mandatory when serving this dish.

1 lb	raw medium shrimp	500 g
1/3 cup	olive oil	75 mL
Half	green pepper, thinly sliced	Half
1 tbsp	sweet paprika	15 mL
1/4 tsp	salt	1 mL
Pinch	cayenne pepper	Pinch
2 tbsp	finely chopped garlic	25 mL
1/2 tsp	dried oregano	2 mL
	Few sprigs fresh parsley, chopped	
	Lemon wedges	

1. Wash shrimp. As carefully as possible, peel off the little legs and belly shell on the underside of the shrimps without removing either the main part of the shell on the topside or the tail. Set aside.

2. In a large frying pan, heat olive oil over high heat for 1 minute. Add green peppers, paprika, salt and cayenne; stir-fry for 1 to 2 minutes or until the green pepper has wilted. Immediately add reserved shrimp; stir-fry for 2 minutes. Add garlic and oregano; stir-fry for 2 more minutes or until the garlic has started to brown and the shrimps are bright pink and springy. Remove from heat.

3. Transfer to a serving dish, garnish with chopped parsley and fit lemon wedges around the dish for squeezing at table. Serve immediately.

FILET OF SOLE WITH CORIANDER PESTO

SERVES 4

Pesto is traditionally linked to basil; but being thoroughly modern, we can take a few liberties. In this dish, the sun-belt tastes of the pesto come from fresh coriander, lime juice and hot chilies. It's a concoction perfected by one of my own food gurus, Amnon Medad — absolutely the best home cook known to me. He uses it on pizza, with grilled vegetables, with pasta (see recipe, page 152) and also as here, with fish. It'll open a new dimension to your notions of filet of sole, adding some zest to the tired, bland taste that so often characterizes "fresh" sole — which, as often as not, means "freshly defrosted"— on this side of the Atlantic.

Preheat oven to 425° F (220° C)
Baking sheet

Pesto

1 cup	packed roughly chopped coriander	250 mL
1/2 cup	grated strong Italian cheese, such as Asiago, Crotonese or aged Provolone (about 2 oz [50 g])	125 mL
1/4 cup	pine nuts	50 mL
2 tbsp	lime juice	25 mL
1 to 2 tbsp	minced fresh hot chilies *or* 1/4 to 1/2 tsp (1 to 2 mL) cayenne pepper	15 to 25 mL
1/4 tsp	salt	1 mL
1/8 tsp	freshly ground black pepper	0.5 mL
1/4 cup	extra virgin olive oil	50 mL
1 tsp	olive oil	5 mL
1 lb	filet of sole (about 4 fillets)	500 g
8	thin strips red bell pepper	8
	Steamed rice as an accompaniment	

1. Make the pesto: In a food processor combine coriander, cheese, pine nuts, lime juice, chilies, salt and pepper; process until finely chopped. With machine running, add 1/4 cup (50 mL) olive oil through the feed tube; continue to process until smooth, scraping down sides of bowl once. You should have about 1 cup (250 mL) of a bright green, dense paste. Divide in half. Store one half for another use, tightly covered, in refrigerator for up to 3 days. Set other half aside.

2. Brush the underneath (darker side) of the fillets with a little oil. Lay on baking sheet, oiled side down. Spread about 1 tbsp (15 mL) of the pesto on each filet covering the entire surface. Bake for 6 minutes, without turning. Remove from oven and divide fillets between 4 warmed plates. Heap 1 tbsp (15 mL) pesto on the middle of each fillet. Decorate with 2 red pepper strips making an "x" on each fillet. Serve immediately, accompanied by rice and, if desired, a vegetable of your choice.

SHRIMP WITH TOMATO AND FETA

SERVES 3 OR 4

The quintessential Greek shrimp dish, this recipe combines the mellow flavors of tomato, onion and lemon with springy shrimps, all covered in feta and broiled. In Greece, the shrimp are broiled in individual clay pots (hence the Greek name, *garides giouvetsi*), but they work just as nicely cooked in a larger ovenproof dish and scooped out as individual portions at table. In either case, it is important to present this dish with its layer of attractively browned feta intact — and, as always, to avoid overcooking the shrimp when stir-frying.

8- or 9-inch (20 or 22.5 cm) round ovenproof dish
Preheat broiler

3 tbsp	olive oil	45 mL
1/4 tsp	freshly ground black pepper	1 mL
Pinch	salt	Pinch
1 cup	thinly sliced onions	250 mL
1 tbsp	lemon zest, cut into ribbons	15 mL
12 oz	plum tomatoes, peeled and quartered, with juices	375 g
1 tsp	dried oregano	5 mL
2 tbsp	lemon juice	25 mL
1 tsp	drained capers	5 mL
1 lb	raw medium shrimp, peeled and deveined	500 g
5 oz	feta cheese, finely crumbled	150 g
	Few sprigs fresh parsley, chopped	

1. In a large frying pan, heat olive oil with pepper and salt over high heat for 1 minute. Add onions and stir-fry for 2 minutes or until softened and starting to brown. Add lemon zest and stir-fry for 30 seconds. Immediately add tomatoes and oregano; stir-fry 2 minutes or until the tomatoes begin to break up and a sauce starts to form.

2. Add lemon juice, capers and the shrimp; stir-fry for exactly 1 minute, turning the shrimp so that they are light pink on both sides and all the ingredients are well mixed together.

3. Transfer contents of the pan to an ovenproof dish, spreading everything into a flat layer. Sprinkle feta crumbles evenly to cover the entire surface. Broil 6 to 7 minutes until the feta is quite brown and the juices are bubbling up around the perimeter of the dish.

4. Bring the dish immediately to table and scoop out portions, garnishing them with chopped parsley.

GARLIC SHRIMP WITH MUSHROOMS

SERVES 2 AS A MAIN COURSE OR 4 AS A STARTER

We've served these shrimp to everyone from Robert DeNiro to our closest friends and they've been a success every time. They're easy to make and, if you can avoid the temptation to overcook them, essentially foolproof. They're not cheap, of course, but you only live once. This recipe works as an appetizer on its own, or as a main course accompanied with rice and a salad.

3 tbsp	olive oil	45 mL
1/4 tsp	salt	1 mL
1/4 tsp	freshly ground black pepper	1 mL
8 oz	raw large shrimp, peeled and deveined	250 g
6 oz	wild or button mushrooms, trimmed and halved	175 g
1 tbsp	minced garlic	15 mL
1 tbsp	lemon zest, cut into thin ribbons	15 mL
3 tbsp	white wine	45 mL
1 tbsp	lemon juice	15 mL
	Few sprigs fresh parsley, chopped	

1. In a large frying pan, heat olive oil, salt and pepper over high heat for 1 minute. Add shrimp and mushrooms; stir-fry actively for 3 minutes or until the shrimp are pink on both sides and the mushrooms are soft.

2. Immediately add garlic and zest; stir-fry for under 1 minute or until the garlic is beginning to color. Add wine and lemon juice; cook, stirring, for 1 minute or until the liquid bubbles. Reduce heat to medium; cook, stirring, for 1 to 2 minutes or until a thick sauce has formed, but before it reduces too much. Remove from heat.

3. Transfer to a serving dish, garnish liberally with parsley and serve immediately.

CALAMARI, TWO WAYS

Calamari (the cosmetic name for squid) is all about texture. A quick crunch, and then a moist, airy meltingness. The lovely thing about calamari is that you can change its texture with different cooking methods: Poached (as in CALAMARI FRICASSEE; see recipe, page 90), it is as buttery as it is easy to make; grilled, it is super crunchy and juicy (especially if not overcooked); and fried, the most popular method, it is oily and rich as heaven. This recipe combines grilled calamari with a small amount of fried (for a little sinfulness) to create a double whammy of textures. It is dressed with a simple sauce that doesn't drown the subtle flavor of the main ingredient.

Preheat grill or broiler

3 tbsp	extra virgin olive oil	45 mL
2 tbsp	minced red onions	25 mL
1 tbsp	drained capers	15 mL
1 tbsp	finely chopped lemon zest	15 mL
2 tbsp	lemon juice	25 mL
	Salt and pepper to taste	
1 lb	cleaned squid, including tentacles (about 6)	500 g
1 tbsp	extra virgin olive oil	15 mL
2 tbsp	all-purpose flour	25 mL
1/4 cup	vegetable oil	50 mL
	Few sprigs fresh basil or parsley, chopped	
	Tomato wedges	

1. In a small bowl, combine 3 tbsp (45 mL) olive oil, red onions, capers, lemon zest, lemon juice, salt and pepper. Mix to distribute, cover and set aside. (The sauce can sit for up to 3 hours, unrefrigerated.)

2. Separate the tentacles from the bodies of the squid. Wash, drain and set aside the tentacles. Slit the bodies as if they were envelopes. Flatten out, wash both sides and dry them. Roll the bodies in 1 tbsp (15 mL) olive oil on both sides until thoroughly coated.

3. Now you must perform two operations in quick succession:
   (a) Dredge the tentacles in flour, shaking off excess through a strainer. In a medium frying pan, heat vegetable oil over high heat for 1 to 2 minutes or until just about to smoke. Fry the tentacles for about 1 minute, turning them to cook all sides (watch out for spluttering). With a slotted spoon, remove tentacles from oil and transfer them to drain on a plate lined with paper towels.

(b) Grill or broil the squid bodies, on one side only for 2 to 3 minutes or until a skewer pierces them easily and they have lost their shine. (When picked off the grill, they will curl; don't worry, this is normal.)

4. Arrange the grilled bodies and fried tentacles on warm plates. Decorate with basil and tomato wedges. Stir the sauce and drizzle some on the squid, offering the rest for additional spooning at table. Serve immediately, providing serrated knives for easy slicing.

CALAMARI FRICASSEE

The poached version of cala-mari can be prepared using flavored water (as in ITALIAN SQUID SALAD; see recipe, page 62) or, as here, using a broth of aromatics and condiments that becomes a sauce for the final product. This dish pro-vides a subtle taste with feathery textures, but it satis-fies and comforts along with the best of them.

1 lb	cleaned squid, including tentacles (about 6)	500 g
3 tbsp	olive oil	45 mL
4	cloves	4
1/2 tsp	salt	2 mL
1/4 tsp	freshly ground black pepper	1 mL
1 cup	thinly sliced onions	250 mL
1	stalk celery with leaves, finely chopped	1
1 tbsp	finely chopped garlic	15 mL
2 tbsp	balsamic vinegar	25 mL
1 cup	fish stock *or* white wine	250 mL
1 tsp	dried basil	5 mL
1 tbsp	softened butter	15 mL
Pinch	sweet paprika	Pinch
1/4 cup	finely diced red bell peppers	50 mL
	Few sprigs fresh basil or parsley, chopped	
	Steamed rice as an accompaniment	

1. Slice squid bodies into 1/4-inch (5 mm) rings. Cut tentacles at their base to halve them. Rinse and set aside.

2. In a large nonstick frying pan, heat oil with cloves, salt and pepper over high heat for 1 minute. Add onions, celery and celery leaves; stir-fry for 2 minutes or until wilted and beginning to color. Add garlic and stir-fry for 1 minute. Add vinegar and stir-fry for 30 seconds or until sizzling. Add fish stock and basil; cook, stirring, for 1 minute or until bubbling actively.

3. Immediately add the reserved squid and reduce heat to low. Cook, stirring, for 4 to 5 minutes for an *al dente* texture or 7 to 9 minutes for a tender tex-ture. Remove from heat and immediately stir in the butter until it is melted.

4. Portion squid, with plenty of sauce over rice. Sprinkle with a little paprika, garnish with red peppers and chopped basil. Serve immediately.

BROILED SCALLOPS ON EGGPLANT PURÉE

SERVES 4

The same eggplant purée that is transformed into *baba ganoush* can be flavored differently and served hot as a bed for meat or seafood. The most famous recipe is called *Hunkar Begendi* (which translates as "the mayor liked it"), involving a weighty bechamel enhancement for the eggplant and a topping of slow-simmered lamb. Here we've lightened the purée considerably and partnered it with chastely broiled scallops to create an unusual and luxurious dish that doesn't break the calorie bank. It's even easy to make — although I'll admit that separating the eggplant pulp from its seed pods will never be one of my favorite pastimes.

Baking sheet
Preheat oven to 450° F (230° C)

1	large eggplant (about 1 1/2 lbs [750 g])	1
1 tsp	vegetable oil	5 mL
1	medium onion, coarsely grated, with juices	1
1/2 tsp	salt	2 mL
1/4 tsp	freshly ground black pepper	1 mL
1/2 tsp	ground nutmeg	2 mL
2 tbsp	extra virgin olive oil	25 mL
2 tbsp	lemon juice	25 mL
1 tbsp	melted butter (optional)	15 mL
1 tbsp	finely chopped fresh basil (or 1/2 tsp [2 mL] dried)	15 mL
1 lb	large sea scallops (about 12 to 16)	500 g
1 tbsp	olive oil	15 mL
	Few sprigs fresh basil and parsley, chopped	

1. Brush eggplant lightly with vegetable oil. Using a fork, pierce the skin lightly at 1-inch (2.5 cm) intervals. Place on baking sheet. Bake for 1 hour or until eggplant is very soft and the skin is dark brown and caved in. Remove from oven and let cool for 15 minutes.

2. Meanwhile, in a nonstick frying pan, combine grated onion with its juices, salt, pepper and ground nutmeg; cook, stirring, over high heat for 2 minutes or until liquid has evaporated. Add 2 tbsp (25 mL) olive oil and cook, stirring, for 1 minute or until just beginning to brown, Remove from heat and set aside in the frying pan.

3. When cool enough to handle, cut off and discard stem and bottom 1 inch (2.5 cm) of eggplant. Peel the eggplant (the peel should come off easily), scraping pulp from the inside of the peel (discard peels). Cut open the peeled eggplant to reveal its many dark seed pods. Using a small spoon, remove and discard as many seed pods as you can. Transfer the remaining pulp to a colander and let excess liquid drain. (Do not push down on solids.)

4. Transfer the drained eggplant to a small bowl. Add lemon juice. Using a wooden spoon, mash and stir the pulp until puréed. Add purée to onion in the frying pan. Add melted butter, if using, and chopped basil; mix and fold until everything is well integrated. Set aside in the frying pan. (The recipe can be prepared in advance to this point, then kept up to 2 hours, covered and unrefrigerated.)

5. Roll scallops in 1 tbsp (15 mL) olive oil and arrange in a single layer on baking sheet. Broil on one side only for 7 to 9 minutes or to your liking (at 7 minutes, scallops will be firm to the touch and moist inside). During the last minutes of broiling, place frying pan with eggplant purée over high heat; cook, stirring, for 1 to 2 minutes or until bubbling.

6. Put pillows of purée in the center of 4 warmed plates. Portion the broiled scallops directly on each purée. Garnish with chopped basil and serve immediately.

SAUTÉED SCALLOPS IN WINE-LEMON SAUCE

SERVES 4

The large sea scallops featured here offer seafood lovers a sense of wonderful luxury. There are no shells to crack, no bones to pick; just little pillows of pure pleasure. As you might expect, they're also expensive — hence our allocation of only 4 oz (125 g) per person — which is why chefs have long been inventing sauces and accompaniments for them. Here's a zesty sauce invented for my ultra-gourmet and gracious friends, Amnon and Marion Medad.

1 lb	large sea scallops (about 12 to 16)	500 g
1/4 cup	all-purpose flour	50 mL
1/4 cup	olive oil	50 mL
1/2 tsp	salt	2 mL
1/4 tsp	freshly ground black pepper	1 mL
1/4 cup	thin strips red bell pepper	50 mL
1 tbsp	finely chopped garlic	15 mL
1 tbsp	lemon zest, cut into ribbons	15 mL
3 tbsp	lemon juice	45 mL
1 cup	white wine	250 mL
1/2 cup	finely diced tomatoes	125 mL
1 tbsp	drained capers	15 mL
2	green onions, chopped	2
	Steamed rice as an accompaniment	

1. Lightly dredge the scallops in flour, shaking off excess through a wire strainer. In a large nonstick frying pan, heat olive oil, salt and pepper over high heat for 1 minute. Fry the scallops for 2 minutes each side or until browned all over. With a slotted spoon, transfer to a bowl. Set aside.

2. Using the same pan (with its leftover drippings) over medium-high heat, add red peppers and stir-fry for 1 minute. Add garlic and lemon zest; stir-fry for 1 minute or until the garlic is starting to brown. Add lemon juice and stir until it sizzles and browns, about 45 seconds to 1 minute. Add wine; cook, stirring, for 3 minutes or until bubbling actively and slightly reduced.

3. Stir in scallops with their accumulated juices and reduce heat to medium. Add tomatoes and capers. Settle ingredients gently into a single layer in the pan. Shake pan and stir gently for 2 minutes or until everything is warm and the sauce has thickened slightly.

4. Portion scallops and sauce beside plain rice and garnish with chopped green onions. Serve immediately.

CHICKEN

Chicken Fournisto with Vegetables   96

Wine-Simmered Chicken with Fennel   98

New World Chicken Cacciatore   100

Chicken Breast Tapenade Bob Dees   102

Chicken with Fig and Orange Sauce   103

Tagine Chicken with Lemon, Olives
and Grapes   104

Chicken Breast Caponata   106

Morrocan Chicken Pie   108

Chicken Livers Marsala   110

CHICKEN FOURNISTO WITH VEGETABLES

"Fournisto" is the Greek term for "cooked in the oven" — which may not sound terribly exotic to North American ears, but growing up in Istanbul (where few homes were equipped with ovens), it signified something special. Every Sunday, the ready-to-bake dish would have to be taken to the local bakery where, for a fee, it would be baked in the late morning (after all the bread was done), then fetched when ready. Not surprisingly, when we moved to Canada and discovered an oven in our apartment, my mother took full advantage of this luxury, feeding me "fournisto" chicken almost daily. Here I expand on her original recipe with some additional vegetables and a shorter bake in a hotter oven. This one-pot meal is easy to serve; if need be, it can be baked, taken out of the oven to wait and then gently reheated (in a 250° F [120° C] oven for 15 minutes) without any loss in quality.

Large roasting pan with lid
Preheat oven to 425° F (220° C)

4	medium potatoes (about 1 lb [500 g])	4
1	yam or sweet potato, scrubbed	1
1 tbsp	vegetable oil	15 mL
4	chicken legs with thighs attached (2 1/2 to 3 lbs [1.25 to 1.5 kg])	4
1	medium onion, peeled and quartered	1
4	cloves garlic, peeled	4
1	green pepper, trimmed and quartered	1
6	plum tomatoes, quartered	6
1 cup	boiling chicken stock	250 mL
2 tbsp	lemon juice	25 mL
1 tbsp	sweet paprika	15 mL
1 tsp	dried oregano	5 mL
1 tsp	granulated sugar	5 mL
1/2 tsp	salt	2 mL
1/4 tsp	freshly ground black pepper	1 mL
	Few sprigs fresh parsley, chopped	

1. Bring a pot of water to a boil. Add whole potatoes and yam; reduce heat to medium and cook for 7 minutes or until barely pierceable. Drain, cut into quarters and set aside.

Recipe continues...

CHICKEN FOURNISTO WITH VEGETABLES (THIS PAGE) ➤
OVERLEAF: SHRIMP WITH TOMATO AND FETA (PAGE 86)

2. Spread oil over bottom of roasting pan. Add chicken legs, potatoes and yams, more-or-less in a single layer (a little overlapping is fine). Fit onion, garlic and green pepper in empty spots. Distribute tomatoes over everything.

3. Stir together boiling chicken stock, lemon juice, paprika, oregano, sugar, salt and pepper. Pour one-half of mixture evenly over the chicken and vegetables (reserve the rest of the stock). Cover roasting pan. Bake undisturbed for 30 minutes.

4. Remove pan from oven. Toss and turn vegetables and baste chicken with the juices. Return to oven and bake, uncovered, for 15 minutes. Remove from oven and reduce oven temperature to 350° F (180° C). Bring the remaining stock to a boil; pour over chicken and stir in. Return to the oven and let bake, uncovered, for 30 to 45 minutes or until the sauce is reduced and the chicken is falling off the bone. Remove from oven and let rest, covered, for 5 to 10 minutes. Garnish with parsley and serve.

≺ GRILLED LAMB CHOPS WITH MUSTARD (PAGE 112)

WINE-SIMMERED CHICKEN WITH FENNEL

SERVES 4

This recipe follows the basic method used for cacciatore and depends for its appeal on the subtle licorice flavor of fresh fennel. Here I've kept the fat content down by using skinless chicken and by frying with only a little oil in a nonstick frying pan. The result is tender chicken with fennel that is still a little crunchy (by using it in large pieces) and a delightful sauce that demands to be mopped up with mashed potatoes or rice on the side.

1	fennel bulb	1
4	chicken legs (2 1/2 to 3 lbs [1.25 to 1.5 kg]), skinned and halved into thighs and drumsticks	4
1/4 cup	all-purpose flour	50 mL
2 tbsp	olive oil	25 mL
1 tsp	fennel seeds	5 mL
1/2 tsp	ground cinnamon	2 mL
1/2 tsp	salt	2 mL
1/4 tsp	freshly ground black pepper	1 mL
2	onions, cut into 1-inch (2.5 cm) wedges	2
1	large carrot (4 oz [125 g]), scraped and cut in 1/4-inch (5 mm) rounds	1
3 cups	white wine	750 mL
2 tbsp	lemon juice	25 mL
1 tsp	dried rosemary, crumbled	5 mL
1 tsp	dried thyme	5 mL

1. Trim the fennel, saving the dill-like leaves and discarding the branches. Cut the bulb vertically into quarters. Trim away the hard, triangular bits of core inside the quarters and discard. Set aside the trimmed quarters.

2. Dredge the chicken pieces in flour. In a large non-stick frying pan, heat 1 tbsp (15 mL) of the oil over medium-high heat for 30 seconds. In batches, cook chicken 3 to 4 minutes per side or until golden. Transfer chicken to a large saucepan, leaving as much oil as possible in the frying pan.

3. Return the frying pan to medium-high heat. Add 1 tbsp (15 mL) oil, as well as the fennel seeds, cinnamon, salt and pepper; cook, stirring, for 30 seconds. Immediately add the reserved fennel, onions and the carrots; stir-fry for 2 to 3 minutes or until a little charred. Transfer contents of frying pan to saucepan with the chicken.

4. Return the frying pan to medium-high heat. Add wine, lemon juice, rosemary and thyme; bring to a boil. Pour over chicken and vegetables; stir to settle ingredients. Bring stew to a boil. Reduce heat to medium-low, cover and cook undisturbed for 30 minutes.

5. Uncover and stir, pushing ingredients into the sauce as much as possible. Continue cooking, uncovered, for 15 minutes or until chicken is tender and the fennel is easily pierced with a skewer.

6. Using tongs and slotted spoon, remove the chicken and vegetables from the sauce and transfer to a deep serving dish. Keep warm in a low oven. Return the pot with the sauce to high heat and boil for 7 to 8 minutes or until sauce is reduced by one-third to one-half, and has a syrupy consistency.

7. Spoon the reduced sauce onto the chicken and vegetables and stir to mix. Portion out onto 4 plates with plenty of sauce. Garnish with fennel leaves and serve immediately.

NEW WORLD CHICKEN CACCIATORE

SERVES 4

Originally a dish that hunters used to incorporate whatever small game they had in the leather pouch, cacciatore requires only two implements: a frying pan and a lidded pot. Here we use a nonstick frying pan and skinless chicken, which allows us to cook the entire thing with little fat, but still retain the lusty, winter-comforting character of cacciatore. I've also made a couple of refinements to improve upon this old favorite, adding orange to the sauce and using peppers and mushrooms as a garnish instead of letting them melt into the dish while it simmers. Just add some *al dente* noodles and a marvellous meal awaits.

4	chicken legs (2 1/2 to 3 lbs [1.25 to 1.5 kg]), skinned and halved into thighs and drumsticks	4
1/3 cup	all-purpose flour	75 mL
2 tbsp	olive oil	25 mL
1/4 tsp	freshly ground black pepper	1 mL
1	large carrot (4 oz [125 g]), scraped and cut in 1/4-inch (5 mm) rounds	1
2	stalks celery, finely chopped	2
2	medium onions, sliced	2
2 tbsp	finely chopped garlic	25 mL
3 cups	chopped peeled plum tomatoes, with juices (about 1 1/4 lbs [625 g]) *or* canned tomatoes	750 mL
1 cup	chicken stock	250 mL
1/2 cup	orange juice	125 mL
4	sun-dried tomatoes, thinly sliced	4
2	bay leaves	2
1 tbsp	orange zest, cut into ribbons	15 mL
1/2 tsp	dried basil	2 mL
1/2 tsp	dried oregano	2 mL
1/2 tsp	granulated sugar	2 mL
3/4 tsp	salt	4 mL
1 tsp	olive oil	5 mL
1/4 cup	thinly sliced green peppers	50 mL
1/4 cup	thinly sliced red bell peppers	50 mL
4 oz	mushrooms, trimmed and quartered	125 g
	Freshly cooked noodles or pasta as an accompaniment	
	Few sprigs fresh basil or parsley, chopped	

1. Dredge the chicken pieces in flour and set aside.

2. In a large nonstick pan, heat 1 tbsp (15 mL) of the oil with black pepper over high heat for 30 seconds. Add carrot, celery and onions; stir-fry for 3 minutes or until everything is oily and wilted. With a slotted spoon, transfer the vegetables to a large saucepan.

3. Return frying pan to medium-high heat. Add 1 tbsp (15 mL) more olive oil; heat for 1 minute or until sizzling. In batches, cook chicken 3 to 4 minutes per side or until golden. Transfer chicken to saucepan on top of vegetables, leaving as much oil as possible in the frying pan.

4. Return frying pan to the medium-high heat. Add garlic and stir-fry for 30 seconds or until shiny. Add tomatoes, chicken stock, orange juice, sun-dried tomatoes, bay leaves, orange zest, basil, oregano, sugar and salt; bring to a boil. Pour over chicken in saucepan, poking the chicken to settle some sauce to the bottom.

5. Bring stew to a boil. Reduce heat to low, cover and cook undisturbed for 30 minutes or until chicken and vegetables are tender. Remove from heat. Stir to mix, cover and let rest 5 to 10 minutes.

6. Meanwhile, in a nonstick pan, heat 1 tsp (5 mL) olive oil over high heat. Add peppers and mushrooms; stir-fry for 3 minutes or until softened and browned.

7. Portion chicken and sauce over freshly cooked noodles. Garnish with some peppers (both colors) and mushrooms; sprinkle generously with chopped fresh basil. Serve immediately.

CHICKEN BREAST TAPENADE BOB DEES

This recipe is dedicated to our publisher, Robert Rose president Bob Dees. He put in a request for chicken with tapenade (olive dip) during the planning session for this book and here's the result. Traditionally, such a dish would have a tapenade simply spread over grilled chicken, but this recipe features a sauce that contains all of the essential ingredients of tapenade and acts as a simmering agent for the chicken itself. The combination is, as you will see, explosive. The various complementary flavors and tastes weave in and out of the sauce, anchored by the sweetness of quickly sautéed chicken.

8 oz	skinless boneless chicken breast cut into 1/2-inch (1 cm) strips	250 g
2 tbsp	all-purpose flour	25 mL
2 tbsp	olive oil	25 mL
1/4 tsp	freshly ground black pepper	1 mL
1 tbsp	finely chopped garlic	15 mL
2	anchovies, minced	2
1 tbsp	lemon zest, cut into ribbons	15 mL
2 tbsp	lemon juice	25 mL
1 cup	chicken stock	250 mL
1/2 tsp	dried thyme	5 mL
8	black olives, pitted and finely chopped	8
	Steamed rice or potatoes as an accompaniment	
1	small tomato, finely diced, with juices	1
	Few sprigs fresh basil or parsley, chopped	

1. Lightly dredge chicken in the flour and set aside.
2. In a large nonstick frying pan, heat oil with black pepper over high heat for 1 minute. Add garlic, anchovies and lemon zest; stir-fry for 10 seconds. Add chicken and stir-fry actively for 2 to 3 minutes or until browned on all sides.
3. Immediately add lemon juice; cook, stirring, for 30 seconds or until sizzling. Add chicken stock and thyme; bring to a boil. Add olives and cook, stirring, for 2 minutes or until the sauce is syrupy. Remove from heat.
4. Transfer to plates alongside rice or potatoes. Apportion sauce equally. Garnish with tomatoes and chopped parsley. Serve immediately.

CHICKEN WITH FIG AND ORANGE SAUCE

SERVES 2 OR 3

Here's a dish that resulted from our experiments in combining the flavors of dried figs, balsamic vinegar and orange juice to come up with something "new." Of course, nothing new is worth having unless it speaks of and improves upon the old. We hope you'll agree that this chicken dish — with its subtle counterpoints of sweet, tart and spicy — is not only delicious, but very much in line with its culinary precursors from France and Italy.

8 oz	skinless boneless chicken breast cut into 1/2-inch (1 cm) strips	250 g
2 tbsp	all-purpose flour	25 mL
2 tbsp	olive oil	25 mL
1/2 tsp	fennel seeds	2 mL
1/4 tsp	freshly ground black pepper	1 mL
1	onion, thinly sliced	1
1	dried fig, thinly sliced	1
1 tsp	balsamic vinegar	5 mL
1 cup	orange juice	250 mL
1/2 cup	white wine	125 mL
	Salt to taste	
	Steamed rice as an accompaniment	
2	green onions, finely chopped	2

1. Lightly dredge chicken in the flour and set aside.
2. In a large nonstick frying pan, heat oil with fennel seeds and pepper over high heat for 1 minute. Add onion and fig; stir-fry for 2 minutes or until softened. Add balsamic vinegar; cook, stirring, for 30 seconds or until absorbed.
3. Immediately add chicken; stir-fry actively for 2 minutes or until chicken is lightly browned. (Be sure to avoid burning figs and onions.) Add orange juice and bring to a boil. Add wine and cook, stirring, 1 to 2 minutes or until sauce becomes syrupy. Season to taste with salt. Remove from heat.
4. Arrange on plates alongside steamed rice and pour sauce over everything. Serve garnished with chopped green onions.

TAGINE CHICKEN WITH LEMON, OLIVES AND GRAPES

SERVES 2 OR 3

The tagine is a two-piece earthenware contraption with which the Moroccans perform the most saucy of culinary magic. Coals glow and spread warmth to the clay pot on the top half of the tagine, peppering with smoke the already-spicy-earthy sauces that simmer within. The concoctions always include meat, a vegetable and plenty of sauce — ideal for sopping up with dark, chewy bread (the sole accompaniment to tagine). The lightest and most heart-warming tagine of all is chicken, cooked here with lemon, olives and grapes. I offer a version that uses only skinless breast meat and cooks up in 15 minutes total time, instead of the original version for whole chicken that takes an hour and a half. I also suggest a nonstick fry-ing pan, because I doubt many of us could get away with a coal-burning cooking device in the apartment.

8 oz	skinless boneless chicken breast, cut into 1/2-inch (1 cm) strips	250 g
2 tbsp	all-purpose flour	25 mL
2 tbsp	olive oil	25 mL
1/2 tsp	ground coriander	2 mL
1/2 tsp	ground cumin	2 mL
1/4 tsp	salt	1 mL
1/4 tsp	freshly ground black pepper	1 mL
1 cup	finely diced onions	250 mL
2	pinches saffron threads *or* 1 pinch turmeric	2
1 tbsp	lemon juice	15 mL
6	thin (1/8-inch [3 mm]) cross-section wheels of lemon, with peel, seeded	6
6	black olives, pitted and halved	6
1/2 cup	frozen peas	125 mL
1 cup	chicken stock	250 mL
16	green seedless grapes	16
	Steamed rice or couscous as an accompaniment	
	Few sprigs fresh coriander or parsley, chopped	

1. Lightly dredge chicken in flour and set aside.
2. In a large nonstick frying pan, heat oil, coriander, cumin, salt and pepper over high heat for 30 seconds. Add chicken and onions in a single layer; sprinkle chicken as evenly as possible with saffron threads. Stir-fry for 2 minutes or until chicken is lightly browned and onions are softened.

3. Add lemon juice; cook, stirring, 30 seconds or until sizzling. Immediately add lemon slices, olives and frozen peas; fold once or twice to mix. Add chicken stock and bring to a boil, stirring. Reduce heat to medium-low and cook, stirring lightly, for about 4 minutes or until the sauce is shiny and syrupy. Stir in grapes; cook for 1 more minute. Remove from heat.

4. Portion alongside plain steamed rice or couscous with plenty of sauce. Garnish with chopped fresh coriander and serve immediately.

CHICKEN BREAST CAPONATA

Eggplant is a magical vegetable that starts out dry and porous as a sponge, then cooks up oily-smooth and sweet, enhancing everything that is served with it, including chicken. Here we combine chicken and eggplant with the usual ingredients of *caponata* (minus the garlic) for a gently perky concoction that pleases the palate without jarring it.

2 cups	peeled eggplant, cut into 1/2-inch (1 cm) cubes	500 mL
3 tbsp	olive oil	45 mL
1/4 tsp	freshly ground black pepper	1 mL
1	medium onion, sliced	1
8 oz	skinless boneless chicken breast, cut into 1/2-inch (1 cm) strips	250 g
2 cups	plum tomatoes, peeled and cut into 1/2-inch (1 cm) cubes *or* canned tomatoes	500 mL
1 tbsp	drained capers	15 mL
1 tsp	dried basil	5 mL
1 tbsp	balsamic vinegar	15 mL
1/4 tsp	salt	1 mL
8	black olives, pitted and halved	8
	Steamed rice as an accompaniment	
	Few sprigs fresh basil or parsley, chopped	
	Grated Romano cheese	

1. Bring a pot of salted water to the boil while peeling and cutting eggplant. (Keep in mind that eggplant doesn't like to wait long after it's cut and will quickly turn brown.) Add eggplant to the boiling water, reduce heat to medium and cook 5 to 6 minutes or until eggplant is tender and softened. Drain and set aside.

2. In a large nonstick frying pan, heat oil and pepper over high heat for 1 minute. Add onion and stir-fry for 1 minute. Add chicken and stir-fry for 30 seconds. Add eggplant; stir-fry 2 to 3 minutes or until the chicken firms up and everything else is shiny and starting to brown.

3. Immediately add tomatoes, capers, basil, vinegar and salt; cook, stirring, for 4 minutes or until tomatoes are breaking up and a thick sauce has formed. Reduce heat to medium, scatter olives, cover and cook for just 1 minute. Take off heat. Let rest, covered, for 5 minutes.

4. Arrange on plates with steamed rice, garnish with chopped fresh basil and a dusting of grated cheese. Serve immediately.

MOROCCAN CHICKEN PIE

Traditionally, this pie (known as *pastilla*) was made with pigeon and enriched with big puddles of butter. Here we use skinned chicken breast cooked in a bare minimum of oil for a result that is much lighter than the original, but still packs a lot of exotic taste.
Served with the traditional garnishes of icing sugar and cinnamon, this sweet-savory speciality of the Kasbah makes for a flavorful opening course or an excellent lunch alongside some juicy salad.

**Baking sheet, lightly oiled
Preheat oven to 350° F (180° C)**

2 tbsp	olive oil	25 mL
1/2 tsp	ground cinnamon	2 mL
1/2 tsp	ground cumin	2 mL
1/2 tsp	salt	2 mL
1/4 tsp	freshly ground black pepper	1 mL
1lb	skinless boneless chicken breast cut into 1/4-inch (5 mm) strips	500 g
1 cup	pine nuts	250 mL
2 tbsp	chopped fresh mint (or 1 tbsp [15 mL] dried, crumbled)	25 mL
2 tbsp	lemon juice	25 mL
2	eggs, beaten	2
1/3 cup	currants	75 mL
8	sheets phyllo dough	8
1/3 cup	olive oil	75 mL
	Sifted icing sugar	
	Ground cinnamon	

1. In a large nonstick frying pan, heat 2 tbsp (25 mL) olive oil, cinnamon, cumin, salt and pepper over high heat for 1 minute, stirring. Add chicken strips; stir-fry for 2 minutes or until chicken is browned on all sides. Remove from heat. Let cool.

2. Transfer the chicken with all its spicy oil into the bowl of a food processor. Add pine nuts, mint, lemon juice and eggs; process for 1 to 2 minutes, scraping down sides of bowl once, until a homogeneous paste forms. Transfer mixture to a bowl. Add currants; mix to distribute well.

3. On a dry surface, layer 2 phyllo sheets one on top of the other, brushing each lightly with olive oil. Put one-quarter of the chicken mixture in the middle, about 3 inches (7.5 cm) from the top; shape the mixture into a 2- by 3-inch (5 cm by 7.5 cm) rectangle. Fold the top flap of the phyllo over the mixture, fold the side flaps over each other and roll up to form a rectangular pie measuring about 2 1/2 inches by 4 inches (6 cm by 10 cm). Repeat with remaining phyllo, olive oil and chicken mixture.

4. Place pies on prepared baking sheet. Brush tops and sides of pies with olive oil. Bake for 20 minutes or until phyllo is golden and crusty. Let rest 5 minutes.

5. With a serrated knife and a sure stroke, slice each pie diagonally into 2 pieces. Arrange on plates (a whole pie if for lunch; half a pie if for a starter). Sprinkle with icing sugar and cinnamon. Serve immediately, accompanied with salad or some fresh fruit, if desired.

CHICKEN LIVERS MARSALA

SERVES 2 OR 3

Chicken livers, once considered a delicacy (just short of the sublime goose or duck livers), have fallen into undeserved disrepute in modern times — largely because of its association with chopped liver, an indigestible combination of overcooked livers with chicken fat and caramelized onions. Here's an attempt to restore some respect for the poor chicken liver. It's a recipe Algis perfected during his stint in the executive kitchens of the Chase Manhattan Bank, where he cooked for the likes of Henry Kissinger and the Rockefellers.

Marsala is a great cooking wine and is also delicious as a digestive; if you can't find any, substitute an equal quantity of red wine sweetened with 1/2 tsp (2 mL) granulated sugar.

12 oz	fresh chicken livers, trimmed	375 g
1/4 cup	all-purpose flour	50 mL
2 tbsp	olive oil	25 mL
1/4 tsp	freshly ground black pepper	1 mL
1 tbsp	finely sliced garlic	15 mL
1 tbsp	chopped fresh rosemary (or 1 tsp [5 mL] dried, crumbled)	15 mL
1/2 tsp	salt	2 mL
1 cup	Marsala wine	250 mL
	Few lettuce leaves, torn	
2	green onions, finely chopped	2

1. Lightly dredge chicken livers in the flour and set aside.

2. In a large nonstick pan, heat oil with pepper over medium-high heat for 1 minute. Add the livers in a single layer; cook the one side for 2 minutes or until browned. Turn and cook the other side for 1 1/2 minutes. Add garlic, rosemary and salt; stir-fry for 1 minute, turning livers often and letting the condiments brown slightly.

3. Add wine and raise heat to high. Cook, shaking the pan and stirring, for about 2 minutes or until the sauce is dark, sizzling and syrupy. Remove from heat.

4. Arrange lettuce pieces on plates. Portion out livers and sauce on the lettuce. Garnish with green onions and serve immediately.

MEAT

Grilled Lamb Chops with Mustard   112

Grilled Lamb Chops with Minted Yogurt   113

Hazelnut Pork Chops   114

Potato and Chickpea Stew with
Spicy Sausage   116

Lentils with Saffron-Scented Meat   118

Braised Lamb with Beans and Dates   120

Cassoulet with Pork and Zucchini   122

Grilled Keftas with Yogurt Mint Sauce   125

Garlic Keftas with Warm Tomato Salsa   126

Beef Stew with Chorizo and Chickpeas   128

Meat-Stuffed Green Peppers with
Yogurt-Cayenne Sauce   130

Savory Lamb Stew with Garlic
and Tomatoes   132

Lamb Stew with Green Peas and Dill   134

Baked Lamb with Orzo   136

Baked Lamb with Prunes   138

Stiffado   140

Spicy Meat and Rice Loaf   142

Individual Lamb Moussaka   144

GRILLED LAMB CHOPS WITH MUSTARD

SERVES 2

Lamb is the preferred meat of Mediterranean gods and nothing makes it more divinely succulent than the quick sear of a barbecue. This recipe uses a full-flavored coating to protect the delicate lamb from the rigors of the grill. While fresh local lamb is obviously the best, even frozen (if slowly defrosted) meat works, since the mustard coating compensates for the loss of flavor.

Preheat grill or broiler

1 tbsp	whole-grain mustard	15 mL
1 tsp	Dijon mustard	5 mL
1 tbsp	olive oil	15 mL
1/2 tsp	dried thyme	2 mL
1/2 tsp	crumbled dried rosemary	2 mL
1/4 tsp	black pepper	1 mL
4	lamb chops, 1 inch (2.5 cm) thick (about 1 1/4 lbs [625 g])	4
	Salt to taste	
1 tbsp	lemon juice	15 mL
	Few sprigs fresh parsley, chopped	
2	green onions, finely chopped	2

1. In a small bowl, stir together the mustards, olive oil, thyme, rosemary and black pepper until smooth. Generously brush both sides of the chops with this mixture and let rest at room temperature for about 30 minutes.

2. Grill or broil lamb chops to your preference (3 to 4 minutes each side for medium rare). Sprinkle salt and lemon juice on the chops. Serve immediately, garnished with chopped parsley and green onions.

GRILLED LAMB CHOPS WITH MINTED YOGURT

Here's another idea for lamb chops on the barbecue, but as different from the preceding recipe as the east of the Mediterranean is from the west. This Levantine interpretation uses thin chops, charred to exuberantly juicy tenderness on the red-hot coals of small braziers in a white-washed courtyard by the seaside. The flavored yogurt acts both as sauce and condiment; together they'll recall for you warm-weather feasting during jasmine-scented nights.

Preheat grill or broiler

6	lamb chops, 1/4 to 1/2 inch (5 mm to 1 cm) thick, about 1 lb (500 g) in all	6
1 tbsp	olive oil	15 mL
1/2 tsp	dried oregano	2 mL
1/4 tsp	freshly ground black pepper	1 mL
1/2 cup	thinly sliced onions	125 mL
1/2 cup	yogurt	125 mL
1	clove garlic, pressed	1
2 tbsp	chopped fresh mint (or 1/2 tsp [2 mL] dried)	25 mL
1 tbsp	lemon juice	15 mL
1 tsp	extra virgin olive oil	5 mL
	Salt and pepper to taste	
1/2 tsp	dried oregano	2 mL

1. Brush lamb chops with olive oil and lay out on a flat plate. Sprinkle with 1/2 tsp (2 mL) oregano and pepper; top with the onions, pressing down into the meat. Cover and let marinate at room temperature for 20 minutes.

2. In a small bowl, combine yogurt, garlic, mint, lemon juice, olive oil, salt and pepper. Mix to integrate well, cover and let rest up to 30 minutes, unrefrigerated. (This sauce can be prepared in advance and refrigerated. It must be allowed a 30-minute "warm-up" to room temperature and a stir before being served.)

3. Grill or broil lamb chops (with any onions that happen to stick on) for 2 to 3 minutes each side or until done to your liking. Sprinkle with dried oregano just before taking off the grill.

4. Spread a thick quantity of the yogurt sauce on each of 2 warmed plates. Transfer 3 chops onto the middle of sauce on each plate and serve immediately.

HAZELNUT PORK CHOPS

SERVES 2

If you're going to have deep-fried food then, as far as I'm concerned, you should go all the way — make it pork. It turns butter-tender inside, and crunchy-nutty outside, a perfect treat for those winter nights when something utterly sinful is just the ticket. The rich pear chutney accompaniment is merely the icing on the cake.

Hazelnut flour is available in many grocery stores; but if you can't find any, just buy raw hazelnuts and grind them fine in a blender or coffee grinder. Frangelico (hazelnut liqueur) is ideal here, but if you don't want to fork out for a whole bottle, use whatever booze you have on hand — rum, brandy or any liqueur.

1 tsp	butter	5 mL
1	pear, cored, peeled and cut in 1/2-inch (1 cm) slices	1
1 tbsp	water	15 mL
1 tsp	whole-grain mustard	5 mL
1	egg	1
1/4 cup	milk	50 mL
1/4 cup	vegetable oil	50 mL
4	pork chops, 1/2 inch (1 cm) thick, about 12 oz (375 g) in all	4
1/2 cup	all-purpose flour	125 mL
1/2 cup	hazelnut flour *or* finely ground hazelnuts	125 mL
2 tbsp	Frangelico or other hazelnut liqueur	25 mL
	Salt and pepper	
	Few sprigs fresh parsley, chopped	

1. In a small nonstick frying pan, melt butter over medium heat. Add pears and sauté, gently turning, for 2 to 3 minutes or until soft and starting to brown. Add water and mustard; gently toss for 1 minute until well mixed. Remove from heat; reserve in frying pan.

2. In a small bowl, beat egg with milk; set aside. In a large frying pan, heat oil over medium-high heat for 1 minute or until quite hot. Meanwhile, quickly dredge the pork chops in the all-purpose flour and dunk them in the egg-milk mixture; dredge both sides in hazelnut flour. Carefully add to hot oil, reduce heat to medium and cook each side 2 to 3 minutes or until golden brown and cooked through. Drain on paper towel.

3. Return pears to high heat; cook for 1 minute or until sizzling. Add Frangelico; cook, shaking the pan, for 1 to 2 minutes or until sizzling and evaporating.

4. Immediately portion out the pears onto 2 plates. Place 2 pork chops on top of the pears on each plate. Season with salt and pepper and garnish with parsley. Serve immediately.

POTATO AND CHICKPEA STEW WITH SPICY SAUSAGE

SERVES 4

During the long winter months, this is the kind of hearty, legume-based stew with which Southern Europeans bring the sunshine back into their homes. The version we present here is virtually foolproof, requiring just a minimum of attention — and little effort if one uses canned chickpeas (washed with cold running water and strained). Leftovers are wonderful, since the flavors will intensify upon reheating the next day. It can be enjoyed as a vegetarian main course (just omit the sausages) or you can experiment with substitutes for the sausage; any stewing meat (pork, lamb or chicken) will work well. In all cases, the stew is wonderful if served with a salad and crusty bread.

1/2 cup	red lentils (*masoor dal*)	125 mL
1 cup	diced peeled potatoes	250 mL
1/2 cup	scraped carrots, cut into 1/4-inch (5 mm) cubes	125 mL
	Boiling water	
1/4 cup	olive oil	50 mL
1 tsp	sweet paprika	5 mL
3/4 tsp	salt	4 mL
1/4 tsp	freshly ground black pepper	1 mL
1/4 tsp	turmeric	1 mL
2 cups	chopped onions	500 mL
1/4 tsp	chili flakes	1 mL
2 tbsp	finely chopped garlic	25 mL
2	medium tomatoes, cut into 1/2-inch (1 cm) wedges	2
2	bay leaves	2
1 tsp	red wine vinegar	5 mL
1/2 tsp	dried oregano	2 mL
1/2 tsp	dried thyme	2 mL
2 cups	cooked chickpeas *or* 1 can (19 oz [540 mL]) chickpeas, rinsed and drained	500 mL
2	dried figs, cut into 1/4-inch (5 mm) cubes	2
1 lb	spicy sausage (such as merguez, chorizo or spicy Italian)	500 g
2 tbsp	finely minced red onions	25 mL
	Few sprigs fresh parsley, chopped	

1. Soak lentils in boiling water to cover for 20 minutes; drain. Bring 5 cups (1.25 L) water to a boil; stir in lentils and cook 5 minutes. Add potatoes and carrots; return to a boil. Reduce heat to medium; cook, stirring very occasionally, for 10 minutes or until the

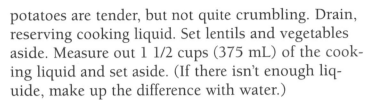

potatoes are tender, but not quite crumbling. Drain, reserving cooking liquid. Set lentils and vegetables aside. Measure out 1 1/2 cups (375 mL) of the cooking liquid and set aside. (If there isn't enough liquide, make up the difference with water.)

2. In a large deep saucepan, heat olive oil over medium-high heat. Add paprika, salt, pepper and turmeric; cook, stirring, for 1 minute, being careful not to let the spices burn. Add onions and chili flakes; cook, stirring, 4 minutes until the onions are soft and beginning to catch on the bottom of the pan. Add garlic and cook, stirring, for 1 minute. Add tomatoes, bay leaves, vinegar, oregano and thyme; cook, stirring, for 2 to 3 minutes or until tomatoes are starting to break up and a sauce forms.

3. Stir in lentil-vegetable mixture, chickpeas, figs and reserved cooking liquid; bring to a boil. Reduce heat to medium-low and cook for 20 minutes, uncovered, stirring occasionally from the bottom up to avoid scorching. Take off heat, cover and let rest for 10 minutes.

4. While stew rests, grill, broil or fry the sausages. Serve stew garnished with sausages, red onions and parsley.

LENTILS WITH SAFFRON-SCENTED MEAT

SERVES 4

Bolstered with additional vegetables, this rib-sticking lentil stew is partnered with meat that is smoky and heady from saffron and garlic. It'll transform even the coldest winter night into an occasion of cozy comfort, especially if served alongside rice and greens. In keeping with our lean and mean, modern tastes, precious little oil (in fact, the bare minimum) is called for here. Therefore, a drizzle of some fine olive oil (chili-spiced if you like) at table will add immeasurably to the appeal of these lentils.

13- by 9-inch (3 L) baking dish
Preheat oven to 400° F (200° C)

1 cup	green lentils, rinsed and drained	250 mL
4 1/2 cups	boiling water	1.125 L
1	carrot, scraped and finely diced (about 1/2 cup [125 mL])	1
1	potato, peeled and finely diced (about 1 cup [250 mL])	1
2 cups	finely diced onions (about 2 medium)	500 mL
1	stalk celery with leaves, finely chopped	1
1/4 cup	finely chopped garlic	50 mL
1 tsp	balsamic vinegar	5 mL
1/2 tsp	dried basil	2 mL
1/2 tsp	dried oregano	2 mL
1 tsp	granulated sugar	5 mL
1/4 tsp	freshly ground black pepper	1 mL
	Salt to taste	
1/4 cup	olive oil	50 mL
1/4 tsp	freshly ground black pepper	1 mL
1/2 tsp	saffron threads	2 mL
1 lb	ground pork *or* lamb *or* beef (or a combination)	500 g
	Salt to taste	
2	medium tomatoes, cut into 1/4-inch (5 mm) rounds (about 1 lb [500 g])	2
	Few sprigs fresh basil or parsley, chopped	
	Extra virgin olive oil	

1. In a large pot, soak lentils in 2 cups (500 mL) of the boiling water for 20 minutes. (They will swell up and absorb most of the water.)

2. Add remaining 2 1/2 cups (625 mL) boiling water. Stir in carrot, potato, 1 cup (250 mL) of the onions, celery, 2 tbsp (25 mL) of the garlic, vinegar, basil, oregano, sugar and 1/4 tsp (1 mL) black pepper. Bring to a boil; reduce heat to medium and cook uncovered, stirring very occasionally, for 45 minutes. (It should have steady but not vigorous bubbles.) By now the lentils and vegetables should be tender, but still holding their shape, and the water mostly absorbed. Season to taste with salt.

3. Meanwhile, in a large frying pan, heat olive oil with 1/4 tsp (1 mL) black pepper over high heat for 1 minute. Add remaining 1 cup (250 mL) onions; stir-fry for 2 minutes or until almost charring. Add remaining garlic and saffron; stir-fry for 30 seconds. Add ground meat; stir-fry, folding to break it up, for 2 to 3 minutes or until no longer pink. Reduce heat to medium-low, cover and cook 3 to 4 minutes or until meat is cooked through and flavorful. Remove from heat. Season to taste with salt; set aside.

4. Transfer cooked lentils to baking dish, spreading them evenly over bottom of dish. Spread the meat and its juices evenly over the lentils. Cover the entire surface of the meat with sliced tomatoes. Bake uncovered for 30 minutes or until the tomatoes have withered and the lentils are happily bubbling.

5. Remove from oven and let rest for 5 minutes. Serve large portions, garnished with chopped herbs, and a beaker of olive oil for drizzling at table.

BRAISED LAMB WITH BEANS AND DATES

Choose a cold winter night and dazzle the loved ones with this sweet-hot stew and its soothing beans and carrots (ideal alongside rice). The sweetness comes from dates (pitted, please), while the heat from crushed chilies provides a necessary counterpoint to the ultimately cloying effect of a sweet-only sauce. If chilies absolutely don't agree with you (a real pity), substitute 1 tsp (5 mL) white wine vinegar (add along with the chicken stock) for a sweet-and-sour result.

2 tbsp	olive oil	25 mL
1/2 tsp	ground allspice	2 mL
1/2 tsp	ground cumin	2 mL
1/2 tsp	salt	2 mL
1/4 tsp	freshly ground black pepper	1 mL
2 cups	finely diced onions	500 mL
1/4 to 1/2 tsp	chili flakes, or to taste	1 to 2 mL
2 1/2 lbs	lamb leg or shoulder cut into in 1 1/2-inch (4 cm) pieces (bone in, fat trimmed)	1.25 kg
1	large carrot, scraped and cut into 1/4-inch (5 mm) rounds	1
2	stalks celery with leaves, finely chopped	2
1 cup	diced peeled tomatoes, with juice *or* canned tomatoes	250 mL
3 cups	boiling chicken stock	750 mL
1 tsp	dried oregano	5 mL
1 tsp	dried thyme	5 mL
1 cup	pitted dates (about 4 oz [125 g])	250 mL
2 cups	cooked white kidney beans *or* 1 can (19 oz [540 mL]), rinsed and drained	500 mL
1/4 cup	packed chopped fresh parsley	50 mL
	Steamed rice as an accompaniment	

1. In a large saucepan, heat olive oil, allspice, cumin, salt and pepper over high heat, stirring, for 1 minute. Add onions and chili flakes; stir-fry for 4 minutes or until starting to brown. Add lamb and cook, stirring actively, for 5 to 7 minutes or until the lamb is thoroughly browned and everything is well mixed together. Add carrot, celery, tomatoes, chicken stock, oregano and thyme; mix together to settle everything in the liquid.

2. Bring to a boil and reduce heat to medium. Cook uncovered for 45 minutes or until the lamb is tender. Stir every 15 minutes and keep up a steady but not vigorous bubble.

3. Fold in dates, beans and parsley; wait for the steady-but-not-vigorous bubble to return. Cook for 20 minutes, folding from the bottom up every 5 minutes to avoid scorching. Remove from heat and cover. Let rest for 5 to 10 minutes.

4. Portion alongside steamed rice with plenty of sauce, and serve immediately.

CASSOULET WITH PORK AND ZUCCHINI

SERVES 6

Baked beans take many forms around the world, and cassoulet is the version favored in the well-fed northern regions of France. There, any number of fatty meats (goose and/or pork fat, for example) are mixed with beans and baked under an equally fatty crust. Here we "Mediterraneanize" the original recipe, using additional vegetables and a lot less fat. Still, this is a hefty and lengthy dish that requires cool weather, a suitable occasion (to justify the effort), and a well-ventilated room.

Deep baking dish, measuring about 12 by 16 inches (30 by 40 cm)

1 tbsp	olive oil	15 mL
1/4 tsp	salt	1 mL
1/4 tsp	freshly ground black pepper	1 mL
1 lb	pork tenderloin, cut into 1-inch (2.5 cm) cubes	500 g
1 tbsp	finely chopped garlic	15 mL
1 tbsp	olive oil	15 mL
1/2 tsp	salt	2 mL
1/2 tsp	freshly ground black pepper	2 mL
1 cup	finely diced onions	250 mL
2	medium leeks, trimmed, washed and finely chopped (about 3 cups [750 mL])	2
2	stalks celery with leaves, finely chopped	2
Half	green pepper, finely diced	Half
1	large carrot, scraped and finely diced (about 4 oz [125 g])	1
8 oz	mushrooms, trimmed and quartered	250 g
1 lb	tomatoes, peeled and finely chopped (about 2 cups [500 mL]) or canned tomatoes	500 g
1 tbsp	tomato paste, diluted in 1 cup (250 mL) water	15 mL
1 tsp	red wine vinegar	5 mL
1 tsp	dried basil	5 mL
1 tsp	dried oregano	5 mL
2 cups	cooked white kidney beans or 1 can (19 oz [540 mL]), rinsed and drained	500 mL
2 cups	cooked red Romano beans or 1 can (19 oz [540 mL]), rinsed and drained	500 mL

| 1 | medium zucchini cut into 1/4-inch (5 mm) rounds (about 8 oz [250 g]) | 1 |
| 2 cups | chicken stock | 500 mL |

Topping

2 cups	breadcrumbs	500 mL
1 tbsp	finely chopped garlic	15 mL
1/2 tsp	ground allspice	2 mL
2	eggs, beaten	2
2 tbsp	olive oil	25 mL
1 cup	dry white vermouth *or* white wine	250 mL
	Few sprigs fresh parsley, chopped	

1. In a large nonstick frying pan, heat 1 tbsp (15 mL) olive oil, salt and pepper over high heat for 30 seconds. Add pork and stir-fry for 2 minutes, turning meat often so that all the pieces are thoroughly browned. Add garlic and stir-fry 1 more minute. Transfer contents of the frying pan to a large saucepan.

2. Return the frying pan to high heat. Add 1 tbsp (15 mL) olive oil, salt and pepper; heat for 30 seconds. Add onions, leeks, celery, green pepper, carrot and mushrooms; cook, stirring, for 4 minutes or until the vegetables are softened and a little oily. Transfer vegetables to saucepan with meat.

3. Stir in tomatoes, diluted tomato paste, vinegar, dried basil and oregano. Bring to a boil, cover tightly, reduce heat to medium-low and cook for 25 to 30 minutes or until the meat is cooked through. Remove from heat.

Recipe continues next page ...

4. Preheat oven to 375° F (190° C). Add white kidney beans, red Romano beans, zucchini and chicken stock to the stew. Gently fold to mix everything thoroughly. Transfer this mixture to baking dish. Spread mixture over bottom of dish, making a layer about 1 1/2 inches (4 cm) deep.

5. Make the topping: In a bowl stir together the breadcrumbs, garlic and allspice until combined. In a small bowl, combine the eggs, olive oil and vermouth. Add this liquid to the breadcrumbs and stir to mix until combined (it'll be wet and lumpy).

6. As evenly as possible, spread this topping over the stew. Bake uncovered for 30 minutes. Remove from oven and press the topping (which will have browned a little) just into the stew, but leaving it still on top. Put back in the oven and bake another 30 minutes until the topping is nicely crusted and the stew is bubbling underneath.

7. Remove from oven and let rest 10 minutes. Portion onto plates, keeping breadcrumbs on top; garnish with chopped parsley and serve immediately.

GRILLED KEFTAS WITH YOGURT MINT SAUCE

SERVES 4

The people of the eastern Mediterranean have invented many savory recipes for minced meat, most of them venerable descendants of original recipes from Afghanistan and Persia. Here is one that is sweetly flavored with parsley and onion, served with a yogurt dressing like that used with GRILLED LAMB CHOPS WITH MINTED YOGURT (see recipe, page 113).

It is important to mix the meat properly (at least 3 minutes of active kneading), and to let it stay in the fridge for 30 minutes, making it firmer and therfore easier to form into patties.

Any salad goes very well with these keftas; for a real treat, serve with homemade French fries.

1 lb	ground lamb *or* beef (or a combination)	500 g
1/4 cup	finely chopped parsley	50 mL
1 tsp	dried oregano	5 mL
1/4 tsp	freshly ground black pepper	1 mL
1	onion	1
1 cup	yogurt	250 mL
2	cloves garlic, pressed	2
1/4 cup	chopped fresh mint (or 1 tsp [5 mL] dried)	50 mL
2 tbsp	lemon juice	25 mL
1 tsp	extra virgin olive oil	5 mL
	Salt and pepper to taste	
	Extra salt	

1. Put minced meat into a bowl and spread it out. Sprinkle with parsley, oregano and pepper. Grate the onion through the grater's largest holes directly onto the meat, so as to catch all the onion juices. Knead the meat and its condiments actively for at least 3 minutes, until everything is well distributed and the meat has paled in color. Cover and refrigerate for at least 30 minutes (or up to 2 hours).

2. In a small bowl, combine yogurt, garlic, mint, lemon juice, oil, salt and pepper. Mix to integrate well, cover and let rest up to 30 minutes, unrefrigerated. (This sauce can wait in the fridge for several hours; it must be allowed a 30-minute "warm up" to room temperature and a stir before being served.)

3. Form the chilled meat into patties just 1/2 inch (1 cm) thick and 2 1/2 to 3 inches (6 to 8 cm) in diameter. You should get 8 of them. Grill, broil or fry them as you would hamburgers (3 minutes each side for medium-rare, 4 minutes for medium, etc.). Serve immediately with salt on the side and the yogurt sauce for spooning at table.

GARLIC KEFTAS WITH WARM TOMATO SALSA

Here's a spicy minced meat specialty which, though heavier than the GRILLED KEFTAS WITH YOGURT MINT SAUCE (see recipe, page 125), has a livelier texture because of its rice filler. In its original form, it is bathed in egg, rolled in breadcrumbs and deep-fried. Here it is made more digestible — as well more succulent and healthier — by grilling it.

The accompanying tomato salsa should be prepared as suggested — hot with chilies. For those who are chili-shy, omit them and still have a good taste. The garlic content, on the other hand, is at its bare minimum. No compromises here.

Accompany with potato salad and some greens for glorious summer feasting.

1/3 cup	short-grain rice	75 mL
1 lb	ground lamb *or* beef (or a combination)	500 g
1 tbsp	minced garlic	15 mL
1	egg, beaten	1
1 tbsp	olive oil	15 mL
1 tsp	ground cumin	5 mL
1 tsp	ground coriander	5 mL
1/2 tsp	ground allspice	2 mL
1/2 tsp	freshly ground black pepper	2 mL
1 tbsp	olive oil	15 mL
1/4 tsp	salt	1 mL
1/4 tsp	freshly ground black pepper	1 mL
1 tbsp	chopped garlic	15 mL
2 tsp	finely chopped fresh hot chilies *or* 1/2 tsp (2 mL) chili flakes	10 mL
1 cup	chopped peeled tomatoes, with juices (about 8 oz [250 g]) *or* canned tomatoes	250 mL
1/2 tsp	dried oregano	2 mL
1/2 tsp	balsamic vinegar	2 mL
	Extra salt	

1. Bring 3 cups (750 mL) salted water to a boil. Add rice, reduce heat to medium and cook, stirring occasionally, for 20 to 25 minutes or until quite soft. Drain. Rinse with cold water, drain and set aside.

2. Put ground meat into a bowl and spread it out. Spread rice over the surface of the meat. Sprinkle with garlic. Pour in egg. Knead a couple of times to distribute ingredients. In a small frying pan, heat 1 tbsp (15 mL) oil over medium heat for 30 seconds.

Add cumin, coriander, allspice and pepper; stir-fry for 1 minute or until aromatic and darkened. Scrape spiced oil onto the meat. Knead the meat and its condiments actively for at least 3 minutes until everything is well distributed and the meat has paled in color. Cover and refrigerate for at least 30 minutes (or up to 2 hours).

3. In a frying pan, heat 1 tbsp (15 mL) oil, salt and pepper for 30 seconds over high heat. Add garlic and chilies; stir-fry for 1 minute or until starting to brown. Add tomatoes, oregano and vinegar; stir-fry for 2 minutes or until the tomato is breaking up and a sauce forms. Reduce heat to medium and cook, stirring, for 2 more minutes or until quite saucy. Remove from heat, cover and let rest lukewarm while you cook the meat.

4. Form the chilled meat into patties just 1/2 inch (1 cm) thick and 2 1/2 to 3 inches (6 to 7.5 cm) in diameter. You should get 8 patties. Grill, broil or fry them as you would hamburgers (3 minutes each side for medium rare, 4 minutes for medium, etc.). Serve immediately with salt on the side and the tomato sauce for spooning at table.

BEEF STEW WITH CHORIZO AND CHICKPEAS

This stew combines French bourguignon technique with the very Spanish flavor of chorizo, whose paprika-garlic essence seems to crop up in just about every kitchen on the Iberian Peninsula. Strictly speaking, this particular combination is purely an invention of mine; once you've tasted it, however, I'm sure you'll agree it has the savor of a heritage recipe. In any case, this dish certainly has been a big favorite on movie sets I've catered during winter shoots — a tribute, no doubt, to its restorative powers, readying the body for a return to the freezing outdoors for more takes of the beautiful Canadian wilderness.

1/4 cup	olive oil	50 mL
1/4 tsp	freshly ground black pepper	1 mL
1 1/2 lbs	lean stewing beef, cut into 3/4-inch (2 cm) cubes	750 g
8 oz	chorizo sausage, cut into 1/2-inch (1 cm) pieces	250 g
2 tbsp	finely chopped garlic	25 mL
1 tsp	sweet paprika	5 mL
1 cup	red wine	250 mL
1 cup	chicken stock	250 mL
2 tbsp	tomato paste, diluted in 1/2 cup (125 mL) water	25 mL
1 tsp	dried oregano	5 mL
2	bay leaves	2
1	potato, peeled and cut into 1/2-inch (1 cm) cubes (about 1 cup [250 mL])	1
2 cups	cooked chickpeas *or* 1 can (19 oz [540 mL]), rinsed and drained	500 mL
1/2 cup	finely diced red onions	125 mL
	Steamed rice as an accompaniment	
	Few sprigs fresh coriander or parsley, chopped	

1. In a large nonstick frying pan, heat olive oil and pepper over high heat for 1 minute. Add the beef and the chorizo (in batches if necessary) and fry, turning often, for 2 to 3 minutes or until the beef is thoroughly seared and the chorizo is sizzling. Transfer the meat to a saucepan, leaving as much of the oil as possible in the frying pan.

Recipe continues...

POTATO AND CHICKPEA STEW WITH SPICY SAUSAGE (PAGE 116) ➤
OVERLEAF: PAELLA RODRIGUEZ (PAGE 168)

2. Return frying pan to high heat. Add garlic and paprika; stir-fry for 1 minute or until starting to brown. Add wine; bring to a boil, stirring. Add chicken stock and diluted tomato paste; keep stirring and bring to a boil. Pour this sauce and all its bits over the meat.

3. Stir in oregano, bay leaves and potato. Bring stew to a boil; reduce heat to medium-low, cover tightly and cook, stirring once every 15 minutes to avoid scorching, for 1 hour (mild bubbles throughout) until the meat and potatoes are tender.

4. Stir in chickpeas; cook uncovered for 5 to 7 minutes. Stir, cover and remove from heat. Let rest for 10 minutes, then portion it alongside rice, garnish with red onions and fresh coriander. Serve immediately.

◄ SPAGHETTI WITH WATERCRESS AND SALMON (PAGE 160)

MEAT-STUFFED GREEN PEPPERS WITH YOGURT-CAYENNE SAUCE

Bell peppers become an affordable treat at harvest time, when they are abundant and cheap. Every autumn, my mother would stuff them in the traditional Greek fashion with meat, rice, onion and dill, bake them in the oven, and serve them with a butter- and cayenne-enhanced yogurt. Her version included 1/2 cup (125 mL) butter, achieving an almost indigestible richness. I've reduced the cooking fat to 1/4 cup (50 mL) olive oil, but have retained the final butter for nostalgia's sake. I've marked it optional, so you can omit it, and sprinkle the cayenne right on the yogurt instead.

Large roasting pan *or* baking dish with lid
Preheat oven to 375° F (190° C)

12	green peppers	12
1/4 cup	olive oil	50 mL
1/2 tsp	salt	2 mL
1/4 tsp	freshly ground black pepper	1 mL
2 cups	finely diced onions	500 mL
1 lb	ground pork *or* lamb *or* beef (or a combination)	500 g
1 cup	diced peeled tomatoes, with juices *or* canned tomatoes	250 mL
1 tsp	granulated sugar	5 mL
1/2 cup	short-grain rice	125 mL
1/2 cup	finely chopped fresh dill	125 mL
3/4 cup	chicken stock	175 mL
1 cup	yogurt, at room temperature	250 mL
1 tbsp	butter (optional)	15 mL
1/4 tsp	cayenne pepper	1 mL
1/4 cup	toasted pine nuts	50 mL

1. Slice a 1/2-inch (1 cm) round (including the stem, if any) from the top of each pepper. Set these aside. (They'll serve later as "lids" for the stuffed peppers.) Trim the cavity of the peppers, discarding seed pod and seeds, without puncturing the walls or bottom of the peppers. Set aside.

2. In a large frying pan, heat olive oil, salt and pepper over high heat for 1 minute. Add onions and stir-fry for 1 minute or until shiny and a little wilted. Add ground meat and stir to break it up; cook for 2 to 3 minutes or until no longer pink. Add tomato and sugar; cook, stirring, for 2 minutes. Add rice and cook, stirring, for 3 to 4 minutes or until all the liquid has been absorbed and everything is well mixed together. Remove from heat and stir in the dill.

3. Stuff a scant 1/2 cup (125 mL) of the meat-rice mixture into each green pepper. (It should be about two-thirds full to allow for expansion.) Place stuffed peppers into roasting pan, fitting the peppers snugly in a single layer. Place the reserved tops on the peppers to act as lids. Add chicken stock around the peppers.

4. Cover and bake 40 minutes, undisturbed. Uncover and bake 30 to 40 minutes more to char the peppers and reduce the liquid. Remove from oven and cover the peppers to let them rest for 5 minutes.

5. Spread some yogurt on 6 warmed plates. In a small pan, heat butter 1 minute or until sizzling; stir in cayenne and remove from heat. Carefully transfer 2 peppers to each plate on top of the yogurt. Drizzle some cayenne butter around and over the peppers, garnish with pine nuts and serve immediately.

SAVORY LAMB STEW WITH GARLIC AND TOMATOES

SERVES 4

Saucy and lusty, this easy stew is like a kiss from the Mediterranean. The garlic, tomato, lamb and herbs go together as naturally as craggy coastlines do with azure coves. This recipe is best when tomatoes are in season and the weather is warm enough to dine al fresco. I've made it in small quantities for my own family, as well as in enormous batches for film crews. Either way, it has yet to fail.

Small roasting pan *or* baking dish with lid
Preheat oven to 350° F (180° C)

2 1/2 lbs	lamb leg or shoulder, cut into 1 1/2-inch (4 cm) pieces (bone in, fat trimmed)	1.25 kg
1/2 cup	all-purpose flour	125 mL
2 tbsp	olive oil	25 mL
1/2 tsp	ground cinnamon	2 mL
1/2 tsp	ground cumin	2 mL
1/2 tsp	freshly ground black pepper	2 mL
1	onion, thickly sliced	1
8	cloves garlic, peeled, whole	8
4	sun-dried tomatoes, cut into thirds	4
1/2 tsp	white wine vinegar	2 mL
1 cup	white wine	250 mL
2 cups	ripe tomatoes, peeled and chopped, with juices (about 12 oz [375 g]) *or* canned tomatoes	500 mL
1 tsp	dried oregano	5 mL
1 tsp	dried thyme	5 mL
2	bay leaves	2
	Salt to taste	
	Boiled or mashed potatoes as an accompaniment	

1. Lightly dredge pieces of lamb in the flour. In a large nonstick frying pan, heat olive oil with cinnamon, cumin and pepper over medium-high heat, stirring, for 1 minute. Add the dredged lamb and fry, turning the lamb, for about 4 minutes or until thoroughly browned.

2. Transfer the contents of the frying pan to roasting pan. Set frying pan aside. To the lamb add the onion (breaking it up somewhat), garlic cloves and sun-dried tomatoes. Stir to distribute.

3.   Return frying pan to medium-high heat. Add vinegar and let sizzle. Add wine and bring to a boil, scraping up solids from bottom of the pan. Let boil for 30 seconds. Add tomatoes, oregano, thyme and bay leaves; cook, stirring, for 2 to 3 minutes or until tomatoes start to break up and mixture boils. Add to the lamb; stir to distribute.

4.   Cover and bake for 45 minutes. Stir and return to the oven, uncovered, for another 45 minutes. Remove from the oven, season to taste with salt, cover and let rest for 5 to 10 minutes. Serve on boiled or mashed potatoes with plenty of the gravy and with portions of the cooked onion, garlic and sun-dried tomatoes.

LAMB STEW WITH GREEN PEAS AND DILL

The lore behind this dish, which the Greeks call *araka*, is that it takes half a day to shuck the peas, and the rest of the day to cook them (until they turn grey and can barely hold their shape). Here we eliminate the shucking with ready-to-cook frozen peas, and reduce the cooking time (2 fairly uncluttered hours) to achieve some texture to go along with the lovely taste. Our short-cuts end, however, with fresh dill — nothing else provides the sweet licorice flavor of this recipe. Fortunately it is available year-round everywhere.

2 tbsp	olive oil	25 mL
1/4 tsp	freshly ground black pepper	1 mL
2 cups	diced onions	500 mL
2 1/2 lbs	lamb leg or shoulder, cut into 1 1/2-inch (4 cm) pieces (bone in, fat trimmed)	1.25 kg
1 1/2 cups	white wine	375 mL
2 cups	chicken stock	500 mL
1 tsp	granulated sugar	5 mL
1 lb	potatoes, peeled and cut into 3/4-inch (2 cm) cubes	500 g
	Salt	
3 cups	frozen peas	750 mL
1/3 cup	packed chopped fresh dill	75 mL
1/2 cup	boiling water	125 mL
1 tbsp	lemon juice	15 mL
Half	red bell pepper, finely diced	Half

1. In a large pot, heat oil and pepper over high heat for 30 seconds. Add onions and stir-fry for 2 minutes or until softened. Add lamb and cook, turning often, for 3 to 4 minutes or until the meat is lightly browned on all sides.

2. Immediately add wine; bring to a boil, stirring. Stir in chicken stock and sugar; keep stirirng and bring to a boil. Reduce heat to medium and cook, uncovered, for 30 minutes on a steady bubble, stirring once in a while and removing any solids that float to the surface.

3. Push meat to the sides of the pot and add potatoes to the sauce in the vacated middle. Cook uncovered for about 45 minutes, turning the potatoes once in a while until they become quite tender. Stir to mix potatoes and meat. Season to taste with salt.

4. Stir in peas, most of the dill and boiling water; cook, stirring, for 3 to 4 minutes or until the bubbles return. Reduce heat a notch to medium-low, cover the pot and cook undisturbed for 20 minutes or until the peas have turned light green and everything is steaming happily. Remove from heat, stir in lemon juice and cover the pot. Let rest for 5 to 10 minutes to develop flavor.

5. Portion out the stew and sauce onto large dinner plates, garnish with the remainder of the dill and the red pepper. Serve immediately.

BAKED LAMB WITH ORZO

Most North Americans think of Mediterranean climes as unremittingly hot and sunny. So you may be surprised to learn that every winter, without fail, it gets freezing cold in Greece. And that's when the orzo is dug out of the storeroom, the meat is purchased (lamb if you can afford it, beef if not), the ovens are lit and the giant *giouvetsi* (earthenware oven dish) is dusted off. What you end up with is a dish not unlike this one, with a spare sauce, rich pasta and melting lamb. It gladdens the heart whatever the location and, frankly, whatever the season.

Large roasting pan with lid *or* clay oven dish with lid

2 1/2 lbs	lamb leg or shoulder, cut into 1 1/2-inch (4 cm) pieces (bone in, fat trimmed)	1.25 kg
1/2 cup	all-purpose flour	125 mL
2 tbsp	olive oil	25 mL
1 tsp	ground allspice	5 mL
1 cup	finely diced onions	250 mL
2 tbsp	finely chopped garlic	25 mL
1 tbsp	tomato paste diluted in 1 cup (250 mL) water	15 mL
1 tsp	dried basil	5 mL
1 tsp	dried oregano	5 mL
2	bay leaves	2
1/2 tsp	salt	2 mL
1/4 tsp	freshly ground black pepper	1 mL
3 cups	ripe tomatoes, peeled and chopped, with juices (about 1 1/4 lbs [625 g]) *or* canned tomatoes	750 mL
2 1/2 cups	orzo (about 1 lb [500 g])	625 mL
	Few sprigs fresh parsley or basil, chopped	
	Grated Romano cheese	

1. Lightly dredge the pieces of lamb in the flour. In a large nonstick frying pan, heat oil with allspice over medium-high heat, stirring, for 30 seconds. Add the dredged lamb (in batches, if necessary); cook, turning the lamb, for 4 minutes or until thoroughly browned.

2. Transfer the contents of the frying pan to a saucepan, leaving as much oil as possible in the frying pan. Return the frying pan to medium-high heat. Add onions and garlic; stir-fry for 30 seconds. Add diluted tomato paste, basil, oregano, bay leaves, salt and pepper; cook, stirring, for 1 minute. Add tomatoes and cook, stirring, for 2 to 3 minutes or until bubbly and saucy.

3. Pour sauce over lamb. Set saucepan over medium heat, cover tightly and cook at a gentle simmer for 45 minutes, stirring at halfway point, until lamb is tender. Let rest, covered, for 10 minutes (or up to 2 hours).

4. Preheat oven to 350° F (180° C). In a large pot of boiling salted water, cook orzo 10 minutes or until *al dente* (but still a bit crunchy). Drain. Spread over bottom of roasting pan. Pour lamb and sauce on top of orzo; stir to mix.

5. Bake, covered tightly, for 45 minutes. Remove from oven and let rest, covered, for 10 minutes. Portion onto warmed plates, garnish with chopped parsley and plenty of grated cheese. Serve immediately.

BAKED LAMB WITH PRUNES

SERVES 4

Here's a culinary notion that has been with us since Byzantine times — sweetly sauced, slow-cooked lamb, partnered with prunes and garnished with toasted almonds. This is comfort food at its best. Admittedly, it takes a while to cook. But then, it doesn't require much work — only a few easy chores at the very beginning. This is the perfect dish for a lazy Sunday, where aromas from the oven waft ever more intensely throughout the house and appetites increase exponentially, until the magic moment of the first bite of caramelized lamb smothered with rich sauce. And don't let the richness worry you: While the traditional recipe calls for about 4 oz (125 g) butter, we use only 2 tbsp (25 mL) oil and an optional tablespoon (15 mL) butter.

10-cup (2.5 L) casserole dish

8 oz	pitted prunes (about 1 1/2 cups [375 mL])	250 g
2 cups	boiling water	500 mL
2 tbsp	olive oil	25 mL
1/2 tsp	ground cinnamon	2 mL
1/2 tsp	ground nutmeg	2 mL
6	cloves	6
1/4 tsp	freshly ground black pepper	1 mL
2 1/2 lbs	lamb leg or shoulder, cut into 1 1/2-inch (4 cm) pieces (bone in, fat trimmed)	1.25 kg
3 tbsp	lemon juice	45 mL
1 tsp	granulated sugar	5 mL
1/2 tsp	salt	2 mL
1 tbsp	softened butter (optional)	15 mL
	Steamed rice as an accompaniment	
1/4 cup	toasted sliced almonds	50 mL
1/4 cup	finely diced red bell peppers	50 mL

1. In a bowl pour boiling water over prunes. Stir to separate. Let soak 15 to 20 minutes. Drain, reserving 1 cup (250 mL) of soaking liquid. Set prunes and reserved liquid aside.

2. In a large saucepan, heat oil with cinnamon, nutmeg, cloves and pepper over high heat, stirring, for 1 minute. Add lamb and cook, turning often, for 6 to 7 minutes or until the meat is browned on all sides. Add lemon juice and cook, stirring, for 1 minute or until sizzling. Add reserved prune soaking liquid, sugar and salt. Bring to a boil. Reduce heat to medium-low, cover tightly and cook at a gentle simmer for 1 hour or until the lamb is tender, stirring it once halfway through for good luck.

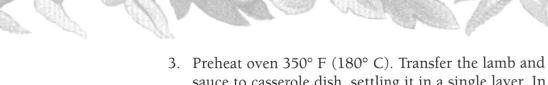

3. Preheat oven 350° F (180° C). Transfer the lamb and sauce to casserole dish, settling it in a single layer. In a bowl toss the optional butter with the prunes. Dot the prunes around the pieces of lamb.

4. Bake uncovered for 45 minutes or until glazed and the sauce is reduced by one-third. Remove from oven and let rest 5 to 10 minutes. Portion out on plates alongside steamed rice, with plenty of sauce. Garnish with toasted almonds and diced red peppers. Serve immediately.

STIFFADO

It is the onions, cooked down to their barest essence, that gives stiffado its reputation for comfort and taste. And it is the onions that present the greatest challenge (that is, extra work) in preparing this dish. Or did I forget to mention that we use pearl onions here? And that they are to be used whole? And that all of them must be individually peeled, without ruining their shape? Well, it's the truth. You cut off the stem and then make a very shallow vertical slit through the skin, which you peel off. And you do this again and again. That's 1 1/2 lbs (750 g) of the little guys to make enough for four.
Still, once you've done that it's a long, clear sail — just simmer and simmer until it's all tender and, oh yes, comforting.

1/4 cup	olive oil	50 mL
1/4 tsp	freshly ground black pepper	1 mL
1/2 tsp	ground cinnamon	2 mL
8	cloves	8
1 1/2 lbs	white or red pearl onions, peeled (see note on technique, at left)	750 g
1 1/2 lbs	lean stewing beef *or* lamb, cut into 3/4-inch (2 cm) cubes	750 g
2 tbsp	finely chopped garlic	25 mL
1/4 cup	water	50 mL
2 cups	ripe tomatoes, peeled and finely diced, with juices (about 12 oz [375 g]) *or* canned tomatoes	500 mL
2 tbsp	red wine vinegar	25 mL
4	bay leaves	4
1 tsp	granulated sugar	5 mL
1/2 tsp	salt	2 mL
	Mashed potatoes as an accompaniment	
	Few sprigs fresh coriander or parsley, chopped	

1. In a large saucepan, heat olive oil, pepper, cinnamon and cloves over high heat for 1 minute. Add onions and stir-fry, turning often, for 2 minutes or until shiny and starting to brown. Add meat; stir-fry for 4 minutes or until the meat is browned on all sides. Add garlic and cook, stirring gently (the onions are beginning to cook; you don't want them to separate), for 1 minute.

2. Stir in water, tomatoes, vinegar, bay leaves, sugar and salt. Bring to a boil. Reduce heat to low, cover and simmer (gentle bubbles) for 30 minutes, undisturbed.

3. Uncover, fold and stir gently. Raise the heat a small notch and cook uncovered for 1 hour or until meat is tender, fold-stirring gently every 20 minutes to avoid scorching (same gentle bubbling throughout). By now the onions will be very soft but still holding their shape. Remove from heat, cover and let rest 5 to 10 minutes.

4. Portion with plenty of sauce along with mashed potatoes. Garnish with chopped coriander and serve immediately.

SPICY MEAT AND RICE LOAF

SERVES 4 OR 5

If the people of the Mediterranean had ever taken it into their heads to adapt the classic North American meatloaf, here's the kind of treatment it would probably have received. Using similar condiments and sauce as for the GARLIC KEFTAS WITH WARM TOMATO SALSA (see recipe, page 126), this dish delivers a summery taste — even in the middle of winter. Leftovers, as always with meatloaf, make excellent sandwiches. This was the favorite dish on the set of *Love! Valour! Compassion!* — a film we catered when it was shooting in the Montreal area. The star of the production, *Seinfeld*'s Jason Alexander, liked it so much that he dubbed us "food gods" (small "g").

9- by 5-inch loaf pan, lightly oiled
Preheat oven to 350° F (180° C)

1 lb	ground beef *or* pork (or a combination)	500 g
1 1/2 cups	cooked rice (from 1/2 cup [125 mL] raw)	375 mL
1/2 cup	grated carrots	125 mL
2 tbsp	olive oil	25 mL
3/4 tsp	salt	4 mL
1/4 tsp	freshly ground black pepper	1 mL
1/2 tsp	allspice	2 mL
1/2 tsp	ground coriander	2 mL
1/2 tsp	ground cumin	2 mL
2 cups	finely diced onions	500 mL
1 tbsp	finely chopped garlic	15 mL
2	eggs, beaten	2
1 tbsp	olive oil	15 mL
1/4 tsp	salt	1 mL
1 tbsp	finely chopped garlic	15 mL
1	fresh hot chili, finely chopped *or* 1/2 tsp [2 mL] chili flakes	1
1 1/2 cups	chopped peeled tomatoes, with juices (about 12 oz [375 g]) *or* canned tomatoes	375 mL
1/2 tsp	dried oregano	2 mL
1/2 tsp	balsamic vinegar	2 mL

1. Put ground meat, rice and carrots in a bowl. Mix a couple of times and set aside.

2. In a large nonstick frying pan, heat 2 tbsp (25 mL) olive oil, salt, pepper, allspice, coriander and cumin over high heat for 1 minute, stirring. Add onions and stir-fry for 2 minutes or until softened. Add 1 tbsp (15 mL) garlic; stir-fry for 1 minute or until garlic starts to brown. Remove from heat and let cool for a few minutes.

3. Add onion-garlic-spice mixture to the meat in the bowl. Add eggs and mix thoroughly, kneading for at least 3 minutes until everything is well distributed and meat has paled in color.

4. Transfer meat mixture into prepared loaf pan and settle it in. Bake for 1 hour.

5. Meanwhile, in a frying pan, heat 1 tbsp (15 mL) olive oil and salt over medium-high heat for 30 seconds. Add 1 tbsp (15 mL) garlic and chili; stir-fry for 1 minute or until the garlic is starting to brown. Immediately add tomatoes, oregano and vinegar; stir-fry for 2 minutes or until the tomato starts to break up and a sauce forms. Reduce heat to medium; cook, stirring, for 3 more minutes or until quite saucy. Remove from heat, cover and let rest lukewarm while you await the meatloaf.

6. Remove meatloaf from the oven. Run a knife along the walls of the pan to loosen the loaf. Hold a large platter over the loaf, and then invert the two together. Tap the pan, and the loaf will fall onto the plate, with its bottom facing up. Immediately slather the tomato sauce across the top surface. Serve to be portioned at table.

INDIVIDUAL LAMB MOUSSAKA

Baked moussaka pie, topped with a cheese-laden bechamel sauce, is a staple of traditional Greek cuisine — and, aside from souvlaki, is probably the highest profile Greek dish on this side of the Atlantic. It derives from a simple Turkish dish that combines meat sauce with fried eggplant, baked until lustrous. I prefer this cheese-free moussaka, probably because I grew up with it in Istanbul.

Baking sheet
Preheat oven to 400° F (200° C)

4	mini eggplants (each about 4 inches [10 cm] long)	4
1 tbsp	salt	15 mL
1/4 cup	vegetable oil	50 mL
2 tbsp	olive oil	25 mL
1/2 tsp	allspice	2 mL
1/4 tsp	freshly ground black pepper	1 mL
1/4 tsp	ground cinnamon	1 mL
2 cups	finely diced onions	500 mL
Half	green pepper, finely diced	Half
2 tbsp	finely chopped garlic	25 mL
12 oz	ground lamb	375 g
1/4 cup	currants	50 mL
1 tsp	dried oregano	5 mL
1 tsp	dried thyme	5 mL
1/2 cup	toasted pine nuts	125 mL
2	ripe tomatoes, cut into 1/4-inch (5 mm) round slices	2
	Few sprigs fresh parsley, chopped	

1. Butterfly the eggplants, cutting them vertically, but not all the way through; spread them open. Immediately sprinkle a thin layer of salt on the flesh sides. (This helps to take away their bitterness.) Let the salted eggplants rest for 10 minutes.

2. Rinse eggplants and pat them dry. In a large nonstick frying pan, heat 2 tbsp (25 mL) of the vegetable oil over medium-high heat for 1 minute. Fry 2 of the eggplants, flesh side down for 2 minutes (careful, they'll splutter); turn and fry the skin side for another 2 minutes. Transfer to a paper towel-lined plate to drain. Add remaining oil to frying pan and cook remaining eggplants. Drain on paper towels.

3. Increase heat to high; return frying pan to heat. Add olive oil, allspice, black pepper and cinnamon; cook, stirring, for 30 seconds. Add onions and stir-fry for 2 minutes or until starting to brown. Add green pepper and garlic; stir-fry for 1 minute. Add lamb and cook, stirring to break it up, for 2 to 3 minutes or until no longer pink. Reduce heat to medium-low. Stir in currants, oregano and thyme; simmer, uncovered, for 3 to 4 minutes. Remove from heat.

4. Lay fried eggplants skin-side down on baking sheet. Distribute pine nuts evenly over the eggplants. Pile meat and sauce evenly on top, spreading out to cover the surface. Top with tomato slices to cover the meat.

5. Bake for 25 to 30 minutes or until the tomato has baked down. Take out of the oven and let rest for 5 minutes. Carefully lift eggplants (they're slippery) onto plates, tomato-side up. Garnish with chopped parsley and serve immediately.

Pasta and Grains

Fettuccine with Fennel and Artichokes   148

Pasta with Spinach and Anchovies   149

Penne with Eggplant and Mushrooms   150

Pasta with Coriander Pesto and Peppers   152

Grilled Polenta with Sausage and Chickpeas   154

Three-Cheese Polenta   156

Mushroom-Spinach Lasagna with Goat Cheese   158

Spaghetti with Watercress and Salmon   160

Rice Pilaf with Apricots and Walnuts   161

Rice and Red Lentil Pilaf with Fried Zucchini   162

Rice and Black Bean Stuffed Peppers   164

Tunisian Couscous   166

Paella Rodriguez   168

FETTUCCINE WITH FENNEL AND ARTICHOKES

Here is a spare-sauced pasta that is quick to make but as elegant as a more belabored creation. The only tricky bit is the final assembly and integration into the sauce, which must be handled carefully (it can be messy) and efficiently so that each portion gets its share of the treats. This recipe can be enriched by adding (at the last minute, in Step 3) cooked chicken strips, pancetta (Italian bacon), sautéed shrimp (or any other seafood), or sautéed mushrooms.

A note on fennel: The fennel bulb always comes attached to woody branches and thin leaves that look like dill. You'll need the leaves for the final garnish, so cut them off and set them aside. Cut off and discard the woody branches. Quarter the bulb vertically, then cut out and discard the hard triangular sections of core. What remains is the usable part of the fennel.

1/4 cup	olive oil	50 mL
1/2 tsp	salt	2 mL
1/4 tsp	freshly ground black pepper	1 mL
1/2 tsp	fennel seeds	2 mL
1	fennel bulb, trimmed, cored and cut into 1/2 inch (1 cm) pieces (about 2 cups [500 mL])	1
1	medium tomato, cut into 1/2-inch (1 cm) wedges	1
4	sun-dried tomatoes, thinly sliced	4
1 tsp	balsamic vinegar	5 mL
1 tsp	dried basil	5 mL
1	jar (6 oz [170 mL]) marinated artichoke hearts, drained	1
1/4 cup	white wine	50 mL
1 lb	fettuccine	500 g
	Shredded sharp Italian cheese (such as pecorino, Crotonese, aged provolone or Romano)	
	Several sprigs fresh basil and/or parsley, chopped	

1. In a large deep frying pan, heat olive oil, salt, pepper and fennel seeds for 1 minute over high heat. Add fresh fennel pieces; sauté for 3 minutes or until the fennel is beginning to color. Add tomato wedges, sun-dried tomatoes, vinegar and dried basil; cook, stirring, for 2 to 3 minutes or until the tomato has broken down and a sauce is forming. Add artichokes and wine, reduce heat to medium and cook, stirring, for 2 minutes or until the sauce is bubbling again. Take off heat and reserve in frying pan.

2. In a large pot of boiling salted water, cook the fettuccine until tender but firm; drain.

3. Return frying pan to medium heat. Add the fettuccine. Toss and combine for 1 to 2 minutes or until all the pasta is coated with the sauce. Serve immediately, garnished with cheese and herbs.

PASTA WITH SPINACH AND ANCHOVIES

Here's a sloppy, jolly pasta for those dinners where decorum is less essential than lusty tastes and comforting textures. The spinach melts into the other ingredients, ending up in clumps of sheer delight that weave in and out of the moistened pasta like perfect harmonies. A word to the anti-anchovy crowd: If you follow this recipe exactly, even the anchovies will become one with the rest of the flavors — only the cook will know it was in there in the first place.

1/4 cup	olive oil	50 mL
1/2 tsp	salt	2 mL
1/4 tsp	freshly ground black pepper	1 mL
1 cup	thinly sliced onions	250 mL
3	anchovies, chopped	3
1 lb	spinach, trimmed, washed and dried	500 g
1 tbsp	drained capers	15 mL
10	black olives, pitted and chopped	10
1 cup	tomato juice *or* vegetable cocktail	250 mL
12 oz	short pasta (such as penne or fusilli)	375 g
	Grated sharp Italian cheese (such as pecorino, Crotonese or Romano)	

1. In a large deep frying pan, heat olive oil, salt and pepper over medium-high heat for 1 minute. Add onions and anchovies; stir-fry for 2 to 3 minutes or until well softened. Add spinach and stir-fry for 2 minutes (it will reduce in volume very quickly), until wilted, and very tender. Add capers and olives; stir-fry for 1 minute to integrate. Add tomato juice and cook, stirring, for 2 minutes or until bubbling vigorously and blending into the sauce. Remove from heat and reserve in the pan.

2. In a large pot of boiling salted water, cook the pasta until tender but firm; drain.

3. Return frying pan to medium heat and add the pasta. Toss and combine for 2 minutes or until there are clumps of spinach everywhere and all the pasta is coated with the sauce. Serve immediately, with cheese on the side for sprinkling to taste.

PENNE WITH EGGPLANT AND MUSHROOMS

SERVES 4

This pasta dish has a messy, peasant look and feel to it, making it ideal for a casual get-together. The sweetness of the boiled-then-sautéed eggplant melts into the sauce, giving the dish its "informal" look, while providing a feast for the tastebuds. The assembly of sauce with pasta in Step 4 requires care and patience to ensure thorough integration.

2 cups	cubed peeled eggplant	500 mL
1/4 cup	olive oil	50 mL
1/2 tsp	salt	2 mL
1/4 tsp	freshly ground black pepper	1 mL
6 oz	wild or button mushrooms, trimmed and halved	175 g
4	cloves garlic, thinly sliced	4
1	medium tomato, cut into 1/2-inch (1 cm) wedges	1
1 tsp	dried basil	5 mL
1/2 tsp	balsamic vinegar	2 mL
1/4 cup	water	50 mL
12 oz	penne noodles	375 g
	Few sprigs fresh basil and/or parsley, chopped	
	Grated Romano cheese	

1. Bring a pot of salted water to the boil while peeling and cutting eggplant. (Keep in mind that eggplant doesn't like to wait long after it's cut and will quickly turn brown.) Add eggplant to the boiling water, reduce heat to medium and cook 5 to 6 minutes or until eggplant is tender and softened. Drain and set aside.

2. In a large deep frying pan, heat olive oil, salt and pepper over high heat for 1 minute. Add mushrooms and eggplant; stir-fry for 3 minutes or until mushrooms are softened and eggplant begins to break up. Add garlic and stir-fry for 30 seconds. Add tomato, basil and vinegar; cook, stirring, for 2 to 3 minutes or until the tomato has broken down and a sauce is forming. Add water, reduce heat to medium and cook, stirring, for 1 minute or until the sauce is bubbling again. Take off heat and reserve in frying pan.

3. In a large pot of boiling salted water, cook the penne until tender but firm; drain.

4. Return frying pan to medium heat. Add the penne. Toss and combine for 1 to 2 minutes or until all the pasta is coated with the sauce. Serve immediately, garnished with cheese and herbs.

PASTA WITH CORIANDER PESTO AND PEPPERS

Here we use the alternative to basil pesto featured in FILET OF SOLE WITH CORIANDER PESTO (see recipe, page 84). Suffice it to say here that, as delicious as it is with fish, it is equally splendid on pasta — and a welcome alternative to the ubiquitous basil pesto accompaniment to pasta dishes. It is very easy to concoct and is certain to impress even those who believe they have eaten enough pesto for a lifetime.

Pesto

1 cup	packed roughly chopped coriander	250 mL
1/2 cup	grated strong Italian cheese such as Asiago, Crotonese or aged Provolone (about 2 oz [50 g])	125 mL
1/4 cup	pine nuts	50 mL
2 tbsp	lime juice	25 mL
1 to 2 tbsp	minced fresh hot chilies *or* 1/4 to 1/2 tsp (1 to 2 mL) cayenne pepper	15 to 25 mL
1/4 tsp	salt	1 mL
1/8 tsp	freshly ground black pepper	0.5 mL
1/4 cup	extra virgin olive oil	50 mL
1 tbsp	olive oil	15 mL
Half	green pepper, cut into 1/4-inch (5 mm) strips	Half
Half	red bell pepper, cut into 1/4-inch (5 mm) strips	Half
12 oz	short pasta (such as penne or fusilli)	375 g
	Grated Romano cheese	
	Extra virgin olive oil for sprinkling	

1. Make the pesto: In a food processor combine coriander, cheese, pine nuts, lime juice, chilies, salt and pepper; process until finely chopped. With machine running, add 1/4 cup (50 mL) olive oil through the feed tube; continue to process until smooth, scraping down sides of bowl once. You should have about 1 cup (250 mL) of a bright green, dense paste. Divide in half. Store one half for another use, tightly covered, in refrigerator for up to 3 days. Set other half aside.

2. In a frying pan, heat 1 tbsp (15 mL) olive oil over medium-high heat. Cook pepper strips 5 minutes or until softened and a little bit charred. Set aside in frying pan.

3. In a large pot of boiling salted water, cook the pasta until tender but firm; drain. Transfer pasta to a warm bowl; add 1/2 cup (125 mL) of the pesto. Stir and toss actively to distribute the pesto evenly. Add the reserved peppers with the pan juices and toss to combine.

4. Serve immediately, with grated Romano and extra virgin olive oil on the side.

GRILLED POLENTA WITH SAUSAGE AND CHICKPEAS

Grits, mumaliga, cornmeal — whatever you call this stuff, it's a highly nutritious and versatile pudding made with milled corn and water. It can be enhanced with anything that strikes your fancy. Here it is broiled with a tiny brushing of olive oil and served on top of a savory sausage and chickpea stew. This dish is easy to make, inexpensive and impressive all at once. Try it, even if you're put off by the notion of consuming anything that can be described as a "pudding." You'll come back to its comforts often, especially in the cold months.

Preheat broiler
Baking sheet

2 1/2 cups	water	625 mL
1/2 tsp	salt	2 mL
1 cup	yellow cornmeal	250 mL
1 lb	Italian sausages (spicy or mild)	500 g
1	onion, sliced	1
Half	green pepper, sliced	Half
1 tbsp	olive oil	15 mL
1 tbsp	finely chopped garlic	15 mL
1/2 tsp	fennel seeds	2 mL
1 cup	finely chopped peeled tomatoes, with juices *or* canned tomatoes	250 mL
1 cup	white wine	250 mL
1 tsp	dried basil	5 mL
2 cups	cooked chickpeas *or* 1 can (19 oz [540 mL]) chickpeas, rinsed and drained	500 mL
6	black olives, pitted and quartered	6
1 tbsp	olive oil	15 mL
	Grated Romano cheese	
	Few sprigs fresh basil or parsley, chopped	

1. In a large deep saucepan, bring water to a rolling boil. Add salt. Reduce heat to low. Add cornmeal in a thin but steady stream, stirring constantly (preferably with a wooden spoon). Cook, stirring, for 2 to 3 minutes or until the mixture is smooth and has thickened to the consistency of mashed potatoes. Transfer the polenta to a medium-sized bowl and cover with an inverted plate. Let rest at least 10 minutes.

2. Meanwhile, broil sausages, onion and green pepper under a hot broiler for 3 to 4 minutes each side. The sausages should not cook through (neither should the onions and peppers burn). Take them out and slice the sausages into 1/2-inch (1 cm) pieces. Mix the sausages, onions and green peppers together; set aside.

3. In a deep frying pan, heat 1 tbsp (15 mL) olive oil over high heat for 30 seconds. Add garlic and fennel seeds; stir-fry for 1 minute or until sizzling. Add sausage, onions and peppers; stir-fry for 1 minute, turning the sausages to sear both sides of the slices. Add tomatoes and stir-fry for 2 minutes to break them up somewhat. Add wine and basil; cook, stirring, for 1 to 2 minutes or until everything is bubbling. Stir in chickpeas and olives. Reduce heat to medium-low, cover and cook for 15 minutes, undisturbed. Remove from heat. Stir, cover and let rest 5 to 10 minutes to develop flavor.

4. Meanwhile, turn cooled polenta onto plate by inverting the bowl and giving it a tap. Cut the polenta into 1/2-inch (1 cm) slices (you should get about 12 slices). Brush baking sheet with 1 tbsp (15 mL) olive oil. Roll each polenta slice in oil on sheet to cover both sides. Arrange slices in a single layer on sheet. Broil polenta slices 6 to 7 minutes, without turning, until crusted and the edges are slightly charred.

5. Divide the stew between 4 plates. Top each with 3 slices of the grilled polenta. Sprinkle with cheese and garnish with basil. Serve immediately.

THREE-CHEESE POLENTA

SERVES 4 TO 6

Here's another recipe for polenta, this time marrying the wholesome cornmeal pudding with three cheeses, tomato, garlic and olives for a high-voltage combination that will warm a winter-weary heart and — a warning here — puts pounds where one might not want them. Calories notwithstanding, I recommend this dish highly for its taste, especially when accompanied by some red wine and followed by a green salad. Ease of preparation also recommends it — the dish can be prepared in advance and baked later. It can also be baked through and reheated (even the next day) without much loss of moisture or flavor.

Deep 6- to 8-cup casserole dish
Preheat oven to 375° F (190° C)

2 1/2 cups	water	625 mL
1/2 tsp	salt	2 mL
1 cup	yellow cornmeal	250 mL
2 tbsp	olive oil	25 mL
1 tbsp	finely chopped garlic	15 mL
1/2 tsp	chili flakes	2 mL
1/4 tsp	salt	1 mL
1/4 tsp	freshly ground black pepper	1 mL
12 oz	plum tomatoes, peeled and roughly chopped *or* 2 cups (500 mL) canned	375 g
1/2 tsp	dried basil	2 mL
1/2 tsp	dried oregano	2 mL
1 tsp	balsamic vinegar	5 mL
4	sun-dried tomatoes, finely sliced	4
4	black olives, pitted and chopped	4
6 oz	low-fat ricotta cheese	175 g
4 oz	Gorgonzola cheese	125 g
3 oz	full-bodied Italian cheese (such as Crotonese, Provolone, Parmesan), shredded	75 g
	Few sprigs fresh basil, chopped	

1. In a large deep saucepan, bring water to a rolling boil. Add salt. Reduce heat to low. Add cornmeal in a thin but steady stream, stirring constantly (preferably with a wooden spoon). Cook, stirring, for 2 to 3 minutes or until the mixture is smooth and has thickened to the consistency of mashed potatoes. Transfer the polenta to a medium-sized bowl and cover with an inverted plate. Let rest at least 10 minutes.

2. Meanwhile, in a frying pan, heat olive oil over high heat for 1 minute. Add garlic, chili flakes, salt and pepper; stir-fry for 1 minute or until the garlic starts to brown. Immediately add tomatoes, basil, oregano and vinegar; stir-fry for 2 minutes or until the tomatoes are breaking down and a sauce forms. Remove from heat.

3. Turn the cooled polenta onto plate by inverting the bowl and giving it a small tap. Spread a small quantity of the tomato sauce on the bottom of casserole. Cut the polenta in half; cut each half into slices 1/4 to 1/2 inch (5 mm to 1 cm) thick. Place half of polenta slices on top of the smear of sauce to make a layer. Scatter sun-dried tomato and olive bits on this layer of polenta. Spread all the sauce evenly. Dot dollops of the ricotta and the Gorgonzola evenly over the sauce. Place remaining polenta slices on top of cheeses. Scatter the shredded Italian cheese on top of the polenta. (The recipe can be prepared in advance to this point and wait up to 2 hours, covered and unrefrigerated.)

4. Bake uncovered for 30 minutes or until lightly browned and piping hot right through. Remove from oven and let rest for 5 minutes. Scoop out portions onto plates, getting some of the shredded cheese layer up top. Garnish with chopped fresh basil and serve immediately.

MUSHROOM-SPINACH LASAGNA WITH GOAT CHEESE

SERVES 4 TO 6

Lasagna layered with meat, cheese and tomato sauce is so much a part of our gastronomic vocabulary that contemplating one with different ingredients requires a considerable stretch of the imagination. Still, there's a world of lasagnas out there. So if you're in the mood for a change, try this meatless variety — it's every bit as satisfying as the original. If expense or calories are a concern, you can substitute low-fat ricotta for the goat cheese in the filling, as well as 12 oz (375 g) low-fat mozzarella instead of the recommended mixture for the topping. For noodles, either cook your own or use the "ready to bake" variety (preferably white ones, to contrast with the spinach).

13- by 9-inch baking dish
Preheat oven to 375° F (190° C)

12 oz	spinach, washed and trimmed	375 g
1/4 cup	olive oil	50 mL
3/4 tsp	salt	4 mL
1/2 tsp	freshly ground black pepper	2 mL
12 oz	portobello mushrooms, trimmed and sliced 1/2-inch (1 cm) thick	375 g
2 tbsp	finely chopped garlic	25 mL
1/2 tsp	chili flakes	2 mL
2 cups	finely diced peeled tomatoes, with juices *or* canned tomatoes	500 mL
1 tsp	balsamic vinegar	5 mL
1/2 tsp	dried rosemary, crumbled	2 mL
1/2 tsp	dried thyme	2 mL
9	cooked lasagna noodles	9
8 oz	goat cheese	250 g
8 oz	shredded mozzarella (about 2 cups [500 mL])	250 g
4 oz	grated strong Italian cheese (such as Crotonese, Asiago or aged Provolone)	125 g

1. In a large pot, bring about 1 inch (2.5 cm) salted water to boil. Add spinach, cover and cook for 1 minute. Uncover, turn the spinach, cover again and cook 1 minute more. Drain. Rinse under cold water; drain. Press lightly to extract more water and set aside in a colander to continue draining.

2. In a large nonstick frying pan, heat 2 tbsp (25 mL) of the olive oil, 1/4 tsp (1 mL) of the salt and 1/4 tsp (1 mL) of the pepper over high heat for 1 minute. Add mushroom slices (they'll absorb all the oil immediately); stir-fry for 3 to 4 minutes or until browned and shiny. Add 1 tbsp (15 mL) of the garlic and stir-fry for 1 minute or until the garlic starts to brown. Transfer to a bowl and set aside.

3. In the same frying pan, heat remaining olive oil, remaining salt, remaining pepper, chili flakes and remaining garlic over high heat for 1 minute, stir-ring. Add tomatoes, vinegar, rosemary and thyme; cook, stirring, until bubbling. Cook, stirring, for 2 more minutes or until the tomatoes are breaking up and a sauce forms. Remove from heat and set aside.

4. Spread the bottom of baking dish with 2 tbsp (25 mL) of the tomato sauce. Lay flat 3 of the lasagna noodles (they should cover the whole surface). Spread the spinach evenly over the surface. Dot half of the goat cheese evenly over the spinach. Cover with another layer of 3 noodles. Spread the mushrooms evenly over lasagna noodles. Dot remaining goat cheese over the mushrooms. Cover with the last layer of 3 noodles and spoon the rest of the tomato sauce evenly over the noodles. Mix the grated mozzarella and strong Italian cheeses; sprinkle evenly over the surface of the lasagna to create the topping.

5. Bake uncovered for 35 to 40 minutes or until the topping is rosy-browned and the inside is bubbling. Remove from oven and let rest, uncovered, for 10 minutes to temper. Lift portions carefully to retain the cheese on top and serve immediately.

SPAGHETTI WITH WATERCRESS AND SALMON

SERVES 4

The fusion of slightly bitter watercress with sweet-salty Gorgonzola and soothing bits of salmon, turns otherwise mundane spaghetti into an inexpensive luxury that is never out of season.

The tossing-mixing in Step 5 can be a bother, especially since it must be done gingerly to ensure that the salmon remains more-or-less intact.

2	bunches watercress	2
1/4 cup	olive oil	50 mL
1/2 tsp	salt	2 mL
1/4 tsp	freshly ground black pepper	1 mL
1 tbsp	finely chopped garlic	15 mL
1 tbsp	lemon zest, cut into ribbons	15 mL
2 tbsp	lemon juice	25 mL
2 cups	boiling chicken stock	500 mL
4 oz	Gorgonzola cheese	125 g
8 oz	skinless boneless salmon, cut into 1/2-inch (1 cm) cubes	250 g
1/3 cup	chopped fresh dill	75 mL
1 lb	spaghetti	500 g
2 tbsp	toasted pine nuts	25 mL

1. Trim the thicker stalks of the watercress and discard. Chop the rest roughly. (You should get about 4 cups [1 L] packed down.) Set aside.

2. In a large deep frying pan, heat oil, salt and pepper over high heat for 1 minute. Add garlic and lemon zest; stir-fry for 1 minute or until garlic starts to brown. Add watercress and stir-fry for 1 minute until it is thoroughly wilted and significantly reduced in volume. Add lemon juice and cook, stirring, for 30 seconds.

3. Stir in chicken stock. Add the Gorgonzola in small dollops; cook, stirring, for 2 to 3 minutes or until the cheese has melted and the sauce is bubbling. Stir in salmon and most of the dill; remove from heat and cover.

4. In a large pot of boiling salted water, cook the spaghetti until tender but firm; drain.

5. Remove cover from frying pan and return to medium-high heat. Cook for 1 minute; add the spaghetti. Toss gently and combine for 1 to 2 minutes or until the pasta is coated with sauce. Serve immediately, garnished with pine nuts and the remainder of the dill.

RICE AND BLACK BEAN STUFFED PEPPERS (PAGE 164) ➤

RICE PILAF WITH APRICOTS AND WALNUTS

SERVES 4 TO 6

A rich, colorful rice that can be eaten on its own as a starter, or on the side of your favorite grilled/sautéed meat or chicken. The dried apricots in the recipe are available just about everywhere and are — despite their name — in fact quite soft and juicy. The saffron, which can be expensive, is easily replaced with the same quantity of turmeric.

3 tbsp	olive oil	45 mL
1/2 tsp	salt	2 mL
1/4 tsp	freshly ground black pepper	1 mL
2 cups	finely chopped onions	500 mL
2 cups	short-grain rice	500 mL
4	sun-dried tomatoes, thinly sliced	4
1/2 cup	thinly sliced dried apricots	125 mL
1/4 tsp	saffron threads	1 mL
4 cups	boiling chicken stock	1 L
1 tsp	olive oil	5 mL
2/3 cup	walnut pieces	150 mL

1. In a heavy-bottomed pot with a tight-fitting lid, heat 3 tbsp (45 mL) oil over medium-high heat for 30 seconds. Add salt and pepper; cook, stirring, 30 seconds. Add onions and cook, stirring infrequently, for about 2 minutes or until softened.

2. Stir in rice; cook, stirring, for 2 minutes or until all of it is coated with oil and heated through. Stir in sun-dried tomatoes and apricots.

3. Combine saffron with boiling chicken stock; immediately add to the rice (watch for splutters). Mix to settle rice evenly in the liquid. Reduce heat to low and cover pot tightly. Cook undisturbed for 20 minutes. Remove from heat. Let rest, covered, for 10 minutes. (It will stay warm and improve for up to 30 to 40 minutes).

4. In a small frying pan, heat 1 tsp (5 mL) olive oil over high heat. Add walnuts and cook, stirring continuously, for 2 to 3 minutes or until slightly charred.

5. Uncover rice. Fluff, folding from the bottom up to distribute all ingredients throughout. Garnish with the sautéed walnuts and serve.

◄ BAKED PEACHES WITH AN ALMOND CRUST (PAGE 173)

RICE AND RED LENTIL PILAF WITH FRIED ZUCCHINI

Most "modern" types of cuisine borrow from a number of cultures to create a brand new dish. And this aromatic rice-and-red-lentil concoction is a perfect example. It could have come from India just as easily as from Turkey, while its fried zucchini garnish is strictly Greek. It entails several different procedures but they're all easy and can be performed at leisure — one by one, not simultaneously. The result is satisfyingly exotic and tasty, a most viable (and healthier) alternative to pasta for a light supper or lunch.

1/2 cup	red lentils (*masoor dal*)	125 mL
1 cup	water	250 mL
1/2 tsp	salt	2 mL
1/4 cup	olive oil	50 mL
1/4 tsp	ground cinnamon	1 mL
1/4 tsp	ground cumin	1 mL
1/4 tsp	turmeric	1 mL
1/2 tsp	salt	2 mL
1/4 tsp	freshly ground black pepper	1 mL
3/4 cup	finely diced onions	175 mL
1/2 cup	finely diced red bell peppers	125 mL
2 tbsp	finely chopped garlic	25 mL
2 tbsp	dried currants	25 mL
1/2 cup	short-grain rice	125 mL
2 cups	boiling chicken stock	500 mL
1	zucchini (about 8 oz [250 g])	1
3 tbsp	all-purpose flour	45 mL
Pinch	salt	Pinch

1. Rinse and drain lentils. Put in a saucepan with water and 1/2 tsp (2 mL) salt. Bring to a boil. Remove from heat; pour into a bowl. Let soak 10 to 15 minutes (the lentils will absorb most of the water).

2. Meanwhile in a heavy-bottomed pot with a tight-fitting lid, heat 2 tbsp (25 mL) of the oil, cinnamon, cumin, turmeric, salt and pepper over high heat, stirring, for 1 minute. Add onions and red peppers; stir-fry for 2 minutes or until beginning to char. Add garlic and currants; stir-fry for 1 minute longer.

3. Immediately drain the leftover water from the lentils; add to pot along with rice. Cook, stirring, for 1 minute or until rice and lentils are coated with oil. Add chicken stock and stir to settle everything evenly in the liquid. Reduce heat to low and cover the pot tightly. Cook undisturbed for 20 minutes. Remove from heat. Let rest, covered, for 10 minutes.

4. Meanwhile, cut the zucchini lengthwise into long, thin (1/8- to 1/4-inch [3 to 5 mm]) slices (you should get 8 slices). Dredge lightly in flour. In a large frying pan, heat 2 tbsp (25 mL) olive oil and pinch of salt over high heat for 1 minute. Add zucchini in a single layer and fry each side for 2 minutes or until golden brown. Transfer to a paper towel-lined plate to drain excess oil.

5. Uncover rice-lentils. Fluff, folding from the bottom up to distribute all ingredients throughout. Put portions onto 4 plates. Garnish with 2 slices of fried zucchini per portion and serve immediately.

RICE AND BLACK BEAN STUFFED PEPPERS

The Greeks stuff just about any vegetable they can get their hands on — from cabbage and vine leaves to zucchinis, tomatoes and eggplants. But peppers are their favorites, especially at harvest time, when they are so affordable. This is an heirloom recipe, which has been fleshed out with the addition of black beans, both for color and taste. These peppers are meant to be eaten at room temperature, when their various flavors really come to the fore. They make a perfect buffet item, especially because they can be (carefully) cut in half to double the number of servings. They also keep well (covered) in the fridge; just let them come back to room temperature before serving.

Large roasting pan or baking dish
Preheat oven to 375° F (190° C)

12	bell peppers, various colors	12
2 lbs	onions, stemmed and peeled	1 kg
1/2 tsp	ground cinnamon	2 mL
1/2 tsp	salt	2 mL
1/4 tsp	freshly ground black pepper	1 mL
1/4 cup	pine nuts	50 mL
1/4 cup	currants	50 mL
1/4 cup	olive oil	50 mL
1 cup	short-grain rice	250 mL
1 cup	diced peeled tomatoes, with juices *or* canned tomatoes	250 mL
1 1/2 cups	boiling water	375 mL
1/4 cup	chopped fresh mint (or 1 tbsp [15 mL] dried)	50 mL
1/4 cup	chopped fresh dill (or 1 tbsp [15 mL] dried)	50 mL
2 cups	cooked black beans *or* 1 can (19 oz [540 mL]) black beans, rinsed and drained	500 mL

1. Slice a 1/2-inch (1 cm) round (including the stem, if any) from the top of each pepper. Set these aside. (They'll serve later as "lids" for the stuffed peppers.) Trim the cavity of the peppers, discarding seed pod and seeds, without puncturing the walls or bottom of the peppers. Set aside.

2. In a bowl, shred the onions through the grater's largest holes (you'll have about 3 cups [750 mL] grated onions and juices). Transfer to a large nonstick frying pan. Add cinnamon, salt and pepper; cook, stirring, over high heat for 5 minutes or until most of the juices have evaporated. Add pine nuts, currants and olive oil; cook, stirring, for 3 minutes or until the onions start to catch on bottom of pan.

3. Immediately add rice; cook, stirring, for 2 minutes or until the rice is thoroughly coated with oil. Add tomatoes and 1/2 cup (125 mL) of the boiling water; cook, stirring, for about 4 minutes or until the tomatoes have broken down and the water is absorbed. Remove from heat. Stir in mint, dill and black beans until well mixed.

4. Stuff a scant 1/2 cup (125 mL) of the rice-bean stuffing into each pepper. (It should be about two-thirds full to allow for expansion.) Place stuffed peppers into roasting pan, fitting the peppers snugly in a single layer. Place the reserved tops on the peppers to act as lids. Add 1 cup (250 mL) boiling water around the peppers.

5. Cover and bake for 40 minutes, undisturbed. Uncover and bake for 30 to 40 minutes more to char the peppers and reduce the liquid. Remove from oven, and cover the peppers. Let them cool down completely (about 1 1/2 hours) before serving.

TUNISIAN COUSCOUS

The national family meal of many North African countries, couscous varies from place to place — although only in the nature of its enhancements. This version, from wonderful Montreal home-cook Aziza Saleb, hails from Tunisia. It is most easily reproduced at home because it entails only 2 operations — making the stew-topping and cooking the couscous (semolina) itself. The full shebang, practised with courtly reverence in Morocco, involves a roasted leg of lamb, a vegetarian version of this stew and grilled merguez sausages, plus caramelized onions and rich couscous, laced with rendered lamb's kidney fat instead of mere butter.

Harissa, the hot sauce I recommend here, is widely available imported in cans. If unable to find it, substitute 1 to 2 tsp (5 to 10 mL) cayenne pepper. Couscous is also widely available, imported in 1 lb (500 g) packages.

2 tbsp	olive oil	25 mL
1 tsp	salt	5 mL
2 cups	finely diced onions	500 mL
3 lbs	lamb leg or shoulder, cut into 1 1/2-inch (4 cm) pieces (bone in, fat trimmed)	1.5 kg
1 to 2 tbsp	*harissa* hot sauce (to taste)	15 to 25 mL
6 cups	tomato juice	1.5 L
8 oz	zucchini, cut into 1-inch (2.5 cm) pieces	250 g
8 oz	cabbage, cut into 1-inch (2.5 cm) chunks	250 g
8 oz	turnip, cut into 1/2-inch (1 cm) cubes	250 g
8 oz	potatoes, cut into 1-inch (2.5 cm) cubes	250 g
4 oz	carrots, scraped and cut into 1-inch (2.5 cm) cubes	125 g
2 cups	cooked chickpeas *or* 1 can (19 oz [540 mL]) chickpeas, rinsed and drained	500 mL
2 1/2 cups	chicken stock	625 mL
2 1/2 cups	fine couscous (about 1 lb [500 g])	625 mL
1/4 cup	butter	50 mL
	Few sprigs fresh coriander or parsley, chopped	

1. In a large pot, heat oil and salt over high heat for 30 seconds. Add onions and stir-fry for 4 minutes or until starting to brown. Add lamb and turn in the oil once. Add *harissa* (a bit everywhere); cook, stirring, for 7 minutes or until everything is well mixed together, the lamb is browned on all sides and the moisture is absorbed. Add tomato juice and bring to boil. Reduce heat to medium-low; cook, uncovered, for 45 minutes with steady but not vigorous bubbles, stirring once in a while. By now the meat should be tender.

2. Stir in zucchini, cabbage, turnip, potato and carrots. Increase heat to medium; cook, stirring once in a while, for 30 minutes or until all the vegetables are tender, but very much holding their shape.

3. Stir in chickpeas and reduce heat to low. Let simmer for a few minutes while you cook the couscous. (This recipe can be prepared in advance to this point; remove from heat, cover and let rest unrefrigerated for up to 4 hours; heat to bubbling and then reduce heat to minimum before proceeding.)

4. In a saucepan, bring chicken stock to a boil. Remove from heat; add couscous in a thin but steady stream, stirring actively with a wooden spoon. (It'll become quite thick.) Stir in butter. Put pan over medium heat and cover; cook 3 to 4 minutes. Uncover and, with a wire whisk, fold and stir from the bottom up for 2 to 3 minutes to fluff and heat the couscous throughout.

5. Put a bed of couscous on warmed plates and top with generous portions of the stew. Garnish with chopped coriander and serve immediately. Alternatively, serve tureens of the stew and couscous with a side bowl of the coriander to which diners can help themselves at table.

PAELLA RODRIGUEZ

SERVES 4

It's hard to say which came first, paella or risotto. Similar as they are in method, however, the end results define — in culinary terms, at least — the essential difference between the Spanish and the Italians. What is basically a flavorful, savory porridge in the Italian kitchen becomes, in its Spanish counterpart, a fiesta of colors and diverse tastes. Paella derives its primary signatures from chorizo (Spanish sausage), saffron and short-grain rice.

There are no truly exact measurements in paella and also no absolutely exact times. This recipe, created by writer and good friend Juan Rodriguez, can be followed to the letter, but as you will see there are moments when you'll have to be the boss: Decide when to stir, when to reduce or increase heat, whether it could use an extra

Continues on facing page ...

Preheat oven to 350° F (180° C)

1 lb	chicken drumsticks (about 4)	500 g
6 oz	chorizo sausage	150 g
1/3 cup	olive oil	75 mL
2 cups	finely diced onions	500 mL
1	green pepper, cut into 1/2-inch (1 cm) squares	1
Half	red bell pepper, cut into 1/2-inch (1 cm) squares	Half
5	cloves garlic, chopped	5
2 cups	short-grain rice	500 mL
1 tsp	saffron threads, crumbled	5 mL
3/4 cup	frozen peas	175 mL
6 cups	boiling medium-strength salted chicken stock	1.5 L
1/2 cup	white wine	125 mL
1/2 cup	clam juice *or* 1/2 cup (125 mL) additional white wine	125 mL
8 oz	cleaned squid, cut into 1/4-inch (5 mm) rings	250 g
8 oz	clams *or* mussels	250 g
1	medium tomato, seeded and cut into 1/2-inch (1 cm) cubes	1
3 tbsp	lemon juice	45 mL
8 oz	raw shrimp, peeled and deveined	250 g
4	canned artichoke hearts, drained and cut in half	4
	Lemon wedges	
	Salt and pepper to taste	

Continued from facing page...

measure of stock; to let it catch a little to the pan (very tasty), but stop cooking before anything actually burns (bitter and unpleasant). Possibly the biggest variable is the kind of pan one uses. A metal pan will conduct heat better and is traditional, but the nonstick type we recommend is safer as it is less likely to burn the rice. When you've put up with all its quirks and mastered it, paella is extremely rewarding. It is as terrific for intimate dinners as it is for larger affairs, and leftovers are excellent the next day. We suggest you try this recipe for 4 to get the hang of it and then multiply the quantities for a large celebratory batch with your friends.

1. Bake chicken drumsticks to almost-but-not-quite done, about 30 minutes. Set aside. Meanwhile, slice chorizo in 1/4-inch (5 mm) rings and cut rings in half to get half-moon pieces. In a frying pan, heat 1 tsp (5 mL) of the olive oil over high heat; add chorizo and cook, stirring often, for 3 minutes or until cooked but before it chars. With a slotted spoon, remove chorizo; set aside. Discard rendered chorizo fat.

2. In a deep nonstick saucepan, heat remaining olive oil over high heat for 1 minute. Add onions, green and red pepper; cook, stirring, for 2 minutes. Reduce heat to medium-high; cook, stirring often, about 8 minutes or until softened, golden, reduced in volume and just beginning to char. Add garlic and sauté 1 minute. Reduce heat to low. Add rice and saffron; cook, stirring, until well coated with oil. Stir in peas and chorizo.

3. Now begins the addition of the liquid and a cooking process of about 40 minutes. It is important to let each addition be absorbed before adding the next, and to keep playing with the heat, so that there is constant bubbling (keep your stock boiling as you use it). Start by stirring in 2 cups (500 mL) of the chicken stock. Raise heat to medium-high. Cook, stirring, for 5 to 6 minutes; as the liquid is absorbed, add wine and clam juice. Cook, stirring, 2 to 3 minutes or until absorbed.

4. Add 1/2 cup (125 mL) of stock and the squid. Cook, stirring, 2 minutes or until absorbed. Add another 1/2 cup (125 mL) stock, the clams and chicken drumsticks. Cook, stirring, 2 to 4 minutes or until absorbed. Stir in tomato. Add stock in increments of 1/2 cup (125 mL) and keep cooking and stirring to absorb each addition for 2 to 4 minutes before adding the next. Test your rice before adding the final half cups of stock. It should be soft but still separate, and the paella should be glistening, a little saucy and beginning to catch a touch on the bottom of the pan. Ideally you will have 1/2 cup (125 mL) of stock left over.

Recipe continues next page...

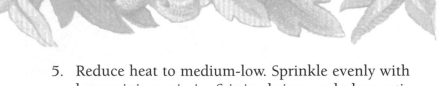

5. Reduce heat to medium-low. Sprinkle evenly with lemon juice; mix in. Stir in shrimp and place artichoke hearts on top of the rice. Cook undisturbed for 1 minute. Take off heat and cover loosely. Let rest for 15 minutes to develop flavor and absorb liquids.

6. Present paella in its cooking pot and let people serve themselves. Pass lemon wedges, salt and pepper for individual seasoning. Accompany with crusty bread and a green salad.

DESSERTS

Glazed Strawberries with Mint   172

Baked Peaches with an Almond Crust   173

Pellegrino Pears   174

Istanbul Almond Cookies   175

Rosewater Pudding   176

Walnut Raisin Cake   177

Greek Honey Cake   178

Almond-Hazelnut Cake   179

Walnut-Chocolate Baklava   180

GLAZED STRAWBERRIES WITH MINT

The appearance of locally grown strawberries heralds the approach of fine weather. And here's a recipe to help you celebrate — a perfect dessert for a deluxe intimate dinner. Of course, modern transport and continual growing in California affords us strawberries even in February; but these are never more than facsimiles of the real thing. Luckily, this recipe will enhance even those strawberries and help bring June to your table throughout the year.

1 tbsp	unsalted butter	15 mL
1 tbsp	granulated sugar *or* maple syrup	15 mL
1 tsp	lemon zest, finely minced	5 mL
16	large ripe strawberries, stemmed	16
1 tsp	lemon juice	5 mL
	Few leaves fresh mint, whole	
	Few leaves fresh mint, chopped	
	Vanilla ice cream	

1. In a medium nonstick pan, heat butter, sugar and lemon zest over high heat for 1 to 2 minutes or until bubbling and clear. Add strawberries; cook, stirring, for 2 minutes or until they are hot to the touch, beginning to stick and most of the liquid has been absorbed.

2. Add lemon juice and stir for less than 1 minute as a reddish sauce forms. Add whole mint leaves and shake pan for 30 seconds to wilt the mint. Take off heat.

3. Portion out onto 2 plates, scraping off the sauce with a rubber spatula. Garnish with chopped mint and ice cream and serve immediately.

Baked Peaches with an Almond Crust

Serves 4

There is no more magical time of year than peach season. It's full summer, the peaches are juicy enough to gag you if you eat them too fast and the days are finally long enough to allow for leisurely, al fresco dinners, where waiting 20 minutes for dessert is actually a pleasure. The almond paste can be prepared in advance, but the peaches must be stuffed and baked to order, and served hot directly from the oven.

Baking dish
Preheat oven to 350° F (180° C)

6 tbsp	ground almonds	75 mL
2 tbsp	brown sugar *or* honey *or* maple syrup	25 mL
1 tbsp	softened unsalted butter	15 mL
2	large ripe peaches (not cling type)	2
1 tsp	softened unsalted butter	5 mL
	Chocolate ice cream and/or raspberry coulis	

1. In a small bowl, combine ground almonds, sugar and 1 tbsp (15 mL) butter, mixing with a spoon to form a paste.

2. Cut a ring around the peaches and neatly separate them in halves. Remove pits. Lightly rub 1 tsp (5 mL) butter all over the peaches to grease the surfaces. Put peach halves in baking dish, skin-side down. Heap a quarter of the almond paste into the pit cavity of each half.

3. Bake the peaches for 20 minutes. Serve (half a peach per portion) immediately, garnished with a dollop of ice cream and/or a smear of raspberry coulis.

PELLEGRINO PEARS

I love poached pears. They're delicious and simple to prepare, requiring only a few basic ingredients and water for poaching. Now, water is normally not a problem. But one day, ready to poach my pears, a municipal plumbing emergency left me with no tap water. What to do? Fortunately, I happened to have (as I always do) my bottle of San Pellegrino mineral water on hand. And thus the happy discovery that mineral water poaches a subtler pear. I've stuck to it ever since. The other requirement of this humble dessert is that it needs time to chill (at least 5 hours) for the best texture and to counterpoint its hot chocolate sauce.

4	ripe unblemished pears	4
3 cups	San Pellegrino mineral water	750 mL
3/4 cup	sugar	175 mL
2 tbsp	lemon juice	25 mL
2	cloves	2
4 oz	bittersweet chocolate, chopped	125 g
8	candied violets *or* candied orange peel (optional)	8

1. Peel pears and cut in half lengthwise; carefully carve out seed pods and discard. Put the pear halves into a bowl; add cold water to cover.

2. In a small saucepan, bring 2 3/4 cups (675 mL) of the mineral water, sugar, lemon juice and cloves to a boil (no need to stir; the sugar melts itself). Drain pears; add to boiling syrup. Cook 30 seconds or until small bubbles appear at the surface; reduce heat to low. Cook, uncovered, 12 minutes or until tender when pierced.

3. Transfer pears and syrup to a bowl; cool to room temperature. Cover bowl and refrigerate for several hours (or overnight) until cold.

4. In a double boiler or microwave, melt chocolate with remaining Pellegrino. When melted, stir with a wooden spoon until velvety smooth. Place 2 pear halves on each plate (cavity-side down) and pour 1 tbsp (15 mL) syrup over them. (The rest of the syrup can be stored to poach another batch of pears, or used to drench a cake.) Mantle each pear half with some chocolate. Serve immediately, decorated with candied violets or orange peel, if desired.

ISTANBUL ALMOND COOKIES

As a child in Istanbul, if I was particularly good, my mother would reward me with some of these cookies. Practically butterless and flourless, they were a lot better for me than, say, a piece of chocolate — and yet much more satisfying. You can turn these cookies into a full-fledged dessert by dressing them with ice cream and any fruit sauce or coulis, but they remain great fun just on their own. Like all cookies, they must be stored in an airtight container.

**Large baking sheet lined with parchment paper
or large nonstick baking sheet
Preheat oven to 350° F (180° C)**

2 tbsp	unsalted butter, melted	25 mL
2	eggs, beaten	2
3/4 cup	granulated sugar	175 mL
1/4 tsp	almond extract	1 mL
2 cups	ground almonds	500 mL
1 tsp	baking powder	5 mL
24	whole blanched almonds	24

1. Brush baking sheet generously and thoroughly with butter.

2. In a bowl whisk together eggs, sugar and almond extract until pale yellow and smooth. Stir in ground almonds until well mixed, thick and sticky. Sprinkle with baking powder; stir until combined. Drop 4 tsp (20 mL) dollops of almond batter onto prepared baking sheet, spread about 1 inch (2.5 cm) apart. Place an almond on top of each cookie; push it into batter to embed it slightly.

3. Bake on the middle rack of oven for 18 to 20 minutes or until edges are brown. The cookies will spread out and touch one another as they bake. Cool for 10 minutes. With a knife, score to separate cookies; lift off with a spatula. Serve immediately while a little warm, or cool completely.

ROSEWATER PUDDING

This simple pudding put the city of Istanbul on the map for back-packers during the 1960s and 1970s. The most affordable of the offerings of the famous "pudding shop" near the train station, it refreshed many impecunious, alternate life-stylers after their lengthy "torture" class (train rides). Rosewater is the dessert's only flavoring and is therefore essential — you can find it in specialty food shops and some pharmacies. It has a taste that some love and some hate. Decide where you stand before you proceed.

Four 1/2-cup (125 mL) dessert dishes

3 tbsp	cornstarch	45 mL
2 cups	cold milk	500 mL
2 tbsp	icing sugar, sifted	25 mL
1 tbsp	rosewater	15 mL
	Crushed pistachios	
	Fresh pomegranate seeds	

1. Put the cornstarch in a small saucepan. Add a little milk and stir until completely dissolved (no lumps). Add the rest of the milk in a stream, stirring. Put the saucepan on medium heat; cook, stirring continuously but not vigorously, for 10 minutes or until steaming, thickened to the consistency of heavy cream and catching a little on the bottom of the pan. Remove from heat.

2. Transfer to dessert dishes; cool completely. Cover dishes; refrigerate for several hours or until cold and set. (A crust will have formed on the pudding's surface.) Serve directly from the fridge dressed with sifted icing sugar and a few drops of rosewater. Garnish with pistachio and pomegranate seeds.

WALNUT RAISIN CAKE

Here's a butterless coffee cake that derives its moistness from raisins and its richness (as well as flavor) from ground walnuts. It is easy to put together — virtually failproof, with the only possible difficulty being that walnuts are one of the few nuts that are not sold pre-ground. The obvious solution is to buy walnut bits and grind them at home in a blender.

If this cake seems a little chaste for your tastes, introduce some sinfulness by using the cake as the base for a slew of gooey, rich toppings such as melted chocolate, ice cream and fruit coulis. It also works splendidly toasted and buttered for tea time or breakfast.

10-inch (4 L) tube pan, oiled and floured
Preheat oven to 350° F (180° C)

1 cup	all-purpose flour	250 mL
5	eggs	5
1/2 cup	granulated sugar	125 mL
1 tbsp	orange zest, finely chopped	15 mL
1 1/4 cups	ground walnuts (about 4 oz [125 g])	300 mL
1 cup	raisins	250 mL
1 tsp	baking powder	5 mL
1/3 cup	freshly squeezed orange juice	75 mL
	Sifted icing sugar	

1. Sift flour; set aside. In a large bowl, beat eggs, sugar and orange zest until frothy and canary yellow. Add walnuts, raisins and flour; do not mix. Sprinkle baking powder on top of the flour; pour orange juice on top of the powder to make it froth. Fold and beat ingredients lightly until incorporated into a thick, homogeneous batter.

2. Transfer into cake pan. Tap it on the counter to settle, and bake for 40 minutes or until risen to twice its original height and cake tester comes out clean. Remove from oven. Let cake cool down completely.

3. Unmold cake by running a knife along both outer and inner walls of the ring. Invert onto a plate. Leave like that to highlight the bottom of the cake where most of the raisins will have descended. Garnish with sifted icing sugar to cover the surface and serve. Store, covered, at room temperature.

GREEK HONEY CAKE

Also known as *revani*, this is the semolina-based cake with which Greeks amuse themselves when the baklava has run out. Easy to concoct — especially if your accomplishments include an acquaintance with beaten egg whites — this version is light and lively. It works spectacularly with serious dairy accompaniments, such as whipped cream, clotted cream or ice cream.

Deep 12-inch (30 cm) round cake pan, lightly oiled and dusted with flour

Preheat oven to 350° F (180° C)

8	eggs, separated	8
1/2 cup	granulated sugar	125 mL
1 tbsp	finely chopped lemon zest	15 mL
1 cup	ground almonds	250 mL
1/2 cup	semolina	125 mL
1 tsp	baking powder	5 mL
3 tbsp	lemon juice	45 mL
1 cup	water	250 mL
1 cup	honey	250 mL

1. In a large bowl, beat egg yolks, sugar and lemon zest until pale yellow and thickened. Add ground almonds and semolina; do not mix. Sprinkle baking powder on top of semolina; pour 1 tbsp (15 mL) of the lemon juice on top of the powder to make it froth. Mix together just until combined.

2. In another bowl, beat egg whites until stiff. Stir about one-quarter of the egg whites into the batter. Add the rest of the egg whites and fold into the batter with circular motions from the bottom up, until mixed thoroughly but not deflated (do not beat).

3. Transfer to prepared cake pan. Bake for 30 minutes or until browned, risen to twice its original height and a cake tester comes out clean. Remove from oven; cool completely on a wire rack.

4. In a small saucepan, bring 1 cup (250 mL) water to a boil. Stir in honey and remaining lemon until dissolved. Return to a boil; reduce heat to medium and cook for 5 minutes, stirring occasionally. Pour hot syrup evenly over surface of cooled cake.

5. Let syrup absorb into the cake; cool once again. Do not unmold. Lift portions directly from the pan onto plates and serve either on its own or garnished with whipped cream or ice cream.

ALMOND-HAZELNUT CAKE

Almonds and hazelnuts are the two poles from which the world of European patisserie is suspended. These two flavorful nuts crop up in myriad guises throughout the sweet-tooth tapestry, which makes our lives ever so slightly more bearable. Here, they are used in tandem and per-fumed with the orangey essence of Grand Marnier (or Cointreau or even a domestic Triple Sec). Ground nuts are available in specialty and health stores and, often, even in supermarkets. If unlucky in finding both kinds of nuts, a full 1 1/2 cups (375 mL) of either will do.

Preheat oven to 350° F (180° C)
10-inch (25 cm) pie plate, lightly oiled
and dusted with flour

3/4 cup	ground almonds	175 mL
3/4 cup	ground hazelnuts	175 mL
1/4 cup	all-purpose flour	50 mL
3/4 cup	granulated sugar	175 mL
1/2 cup	unsalted butter, melted	125 mL
3	eggs, beaten	3
1/4 cup	Grand Marnier or other orange-flavored liqueur	50 mL
1/2 tsp	baking powder	2 mL
	Whipping (35%) cream and/or fruit coulis (optional)	

1. Put ground almonds and ground hazelnuts into a food processor. Sift flour right on the nuts. Add sugar and melted butter. Pulse a couple of times, then scrape down sides of bowl and process until well mixed and sticky. Add eggs and Grand Marnier; process until consistency is like very thick cream. Sprinkle with baking powder; pulse a few times until blended.

2. Transfer mixture to pie plate, tapping plate a couple of times to settle its contents. Bake for 35 to 40 minutes or until the top has browned, the sides have pulled in a little and cake tester comes out almost dry. Remove from oven and let cool down completely in the pie plate (the center will cave in very slightly). Serve wedges from the pie plate directly onto pools of the optional cream, with a light fruit coulis (peach, apricot, strawberry), or on its own.

WALNUT-CHOCOLATE BAKLAVA

SERVES 16

The addition of chocolate gives a new taste to baklava and I thought we should offer a recipe before everyone else does it. Here I use the same slow-cooked, sparely-used-phyllo way that I make all my baklavas. It is just more airy and crunchy than with the more traditional layered-pie method — closer to the feeling of a Middle-Eastern baklava than a Greek one. The better the quality of chocolate you use, the more delicious it'll end up (obviously), but commercial chocolate chips will work, as long as they are semi-sweet.

Rectangular baking dish (about 10 by 16 inches (25 by 45 cm), lightly buttered
Preheat oven to 275° F (140° C)

1 1/4 cups	walnut pieces	300 mL
7 oz	bittersweet chocolate, chopped	200 g
8	sheets phyllo dough	8
1/2 cup	unsalted butter, melted	125 mL
1/2 cup	granulated sugar	125 mL
1/2 cup	water	125 mL

1. Put walnuts and chocolate pieces in the bowl of a food processor. Process at high speed for about 1 minute or until nuts and chocolate are ground to the consistency of coarse meal, with some little chunks left.

2. On a dry working surface, lay out a sheet of phyllo, short side towards you. Using a pastry brush lightly butter the half nearest you. Fold the unbuttered half over and lightly butter the fresh surface. (You'll now have a double layer of phyllo, buttered in-between and above.) Sprinkle 1/4 cup (50 mL) of the walnut-chocolate mixture evenly over the entire phyllo surface. Roll the stuffed phyllo away from you, forming a long tubular shape, a bit more than 1 inch (2.5 cm) wide. This rolling should be as tight as possible, but loose enough so as not to tear the phyllo. Place this tube against one of the walls of the baking dish.

3. Repeat procedure with remaining 7 sheets of phyllo, fitting the new tubes snugly against each other, but without squeezing. When all 8 baklavas have been rolled, they'll fill out the entire pan. There should be just enough butter left over to brush the entire top surface of all the baklavas. This final buttering is very important; if you've run out of butter, then melt some more.

4. Bake the baklavas for 50 minutes or until browned and their surfaces are very crisp. Remove from oven. In a small pan, combine sugar and water; bring to a boil (no need to stir, the sugar melts itself). Reduce heat to medium; cook for 3 minutes or until slightly thickened. Pour hot syrup evenly over the warm baklavas. Let rest for 1 hour.

5. The baklavas can be served at this point or they can sit for up to 2 days, unrefrigerated and lightly covered. Serve half a tube per person, either as is, or cut on the bias into 2 or 3 pieces.

INDEX

A

Almonds:
  about, 19
  cookies, 175
  -hazelnut cake, 179
Anchovies, pasta with spinach, 149
Aromatic fish soup, 70-1
Artichoke hearts:
  about, 55
  fettuccine and fennel with, 148
  green bean and mushroom stir-fry, 23
  paella, 168-70
  salad, 55
Arugula-bocconcini salad, 52
Asparagus:
  and goat cheese flan, 44
  and scallops gratin, 42-3
Avocado:
  and lettuce salad, 50
  and smoked salmon salad, 63

B

Baked lamb:
  with orzo, 136-7
  with prunes, 138-9

Baked peaches with an almond crust, 173
Baklava, walnut-chocolate, 180-1
Balsamic vinegar, about, 15-16
Bay scallops. *See* Scallops
Beans, about, 17
Beef:
  ground,
    green peppers stuffed with, 130-1
    with lentils, 118-19
    meat and rice loaf, 142-3
    with warm tomato salsa, 126-7
  stew, with chorizo and chickpeas, 128-9
Bell peppers:
  grilled leeks with feta and, 36-7
  meat-stuffed with yogurt-cayenne sauce, 130-1
  pasta with coriander pesto and, 152-3
  and seafood salad, 66-7
  stuffed with rice and black beans, 164-5
Bitter greens with paprika, 22
Black beans, and rice-stuffed peppers, 164-5
Black olives:
  about, 16
  chicken breast tapenade, 102

Black olives (continued):
  fish with bell peppers and, 72
  and grapefruit salad, 59
  pasta with spinach and
    anchovies, 149
  tapenade, 38-9
Bocconcini:
  and arugula salad, 52
  broccoli gratin, 28
Braised endive and tomato
  gratinée, 25
Braised green beans and fennel,
  24
Braised lamb with beans and
  dates, 120-1
Broccoli gratin, 28
Broiled halibut with black butter,
  73
Broiled salmon with green
  tapenade and endive, 74-5
Broiled scallops on eggplant
  purée, 92-3
Bruschetta tapenade, 38-9

C

Cake:
  almond-hazelnut, 179
  Greek honey, 178
  walnut raisin, 177
Calamari:
  about, 18
  fricassee, 90-1
  two ways, 88-9
  See also Squid

Capers, about, 16-17
Cassoulet with pork and
  zucchini, 122-4
Cauliflower salad, 56-7
Cheese, braised endive and
  tomato gratinée, 25
  See also specific cheeses
Cherry tomatoes, with cod, 46-7
Chicken:
  breasts,
    caponata, 106-7
    with fig and orange sauce,
     103
    pie, 108-9
    salad, 60-1
    tagine, 104-5
    tapenade Bob Dees, 102
  legs,
    cacciatore, 100-1
    fournisto with vegetables, 96-7
    paella, 168-70
    simmered in wine, 98-9
Chicken livers Marsala, 110
Chickpeas:
  beef stew with chorizo, 128-9
  polenta with sausage, 154-5
  and potato stew with sausage,
    116-17
  Tunisian couscous, 166-7
Chilies, about, 20
Chorizo sausage:
  beef stew with chickpeas and,
    128-9
  paella, 168-70

Clams, paella, 168-70

Cod:

with cherry tomatoes, 46-7

fish soup, 70-1

with peppers and olives, 72

Cookies, almond, 175

Coriander pesto, 84-5

pasta with, 152-3

Cornmeal:

polenta with sausage and
chickpeas, 154-5

three-cheese polenta, 156-7

Couscous, Tunisian-style, 166-7

Crème fraîche, 64

Crusted cod with cherry
tomatoes, 46-7

Crusted salmon with green
peppercorn sauce, 76-7

Cucumber, yogurt salad, 32-3

D

Dandelion greens, with paprika, 22

Daniaile's "little" cauliflower
salad, 56-7

E

Eggplant:

about, 18-19

and broiled scallops, 92-3

chicken breast caponata, 106-7

moussaka, 144-5

and mushrooms with penne,
150-1

Eggplant (continued):

salad, 26-7

Eggs, asparagus and goat cheese
flan, 44

Endive:

salmon with tapenade, 74-5

and tomato gratinée, 25

F

Fennel:

about, 18, 24

chicken simmered with, 98-9

fettuccine and artichokes with,
148

and green beans braised, 24

Feta cheese:

with leeks, 36-7

lettuce and avocado salad, 50

phyllo nests, 41

shrimp with, 86

white kidney bean and tomato
salad, 53

Fettuccine, with fennel and
artichokes, 148

Filet of sole with coriander pesto,
84-5

Fish:

with peppers and olives, 72

soup, 70-1

See also specific fish

Flan, asparagus and goat cheese,
44

Flash-fried red snapper with
green onions, 82

G

Garlic:

  about, 15

  keftas with warm tomato salsa, 126-7

  shrimp with mushrooms, 87

Glazed strawberries with mint, 172

Goat cheese:

  and asparagus flan, 44

  mushroom-spinach lasagna, 158-9

  phyllo nests with cashews, 40

  portobello mushrooms with, 30-1

Gorgonzola cheese:

  spaghetti with watercress and salmon, 160

  three cheese polenta, 156-7

Grapefruit, and black olive salad, 59

Greek-style:

  honey cake, 178

  kidney beans and tomato salad, 53

Green beans:

  and fennel braised, 24

  and mushrooms stir-fry, 23

Green lentils:

  about, 17

  with saffron-scented meat, 118-19

  with spicy sausage, 34

Green peas, lamb stew with, 134-5

Green peppers. *See* Bell peppers

Greens, with paprika, 22

Grilled fresh sardines with red onion sauce, 48

Grilled keftas with yogurt mint sauce, 125

Grilled lamb chops:

  with minted yogurt, 113

  with mustard, 112

Grilled leeks with feta and red pepper, 36-7

Grilled polenta with sausage and chickpeas, 154-5

H

Halibut:

  broiled with black butter, 73

  fish soup, 70-1

  with peppers and olives, 72

Harissa hot sauce, about, 166

Hazelnuts:

  about, 19

  pork chops, 114-15

  to roast raw, 60

Herbs, about, 20

Honey cake, 178

I

Istanbul almond cookies, 175

Istanbul leeks, 54

Italian cheese:

  mushroom-spinach lasagna, 158-9

Italian cheese (continued):

three-cheese polenta, 156-7

Italian sausage, 35

polenta with chickpeas, 154-5

Italian squid salad, 62

J

Jane's chicken salad, 60-1

K

Kebabs, swordfish, 79

Kidney beans. *See* White kidney beans

L

Lamb:

about, 17

chops,

with minted yogurt, 113

with mustard, 112

ground,

green peppers stuffed with, 130-1

with lentils, 118-19

moussaka, 144-5

with warm tomato salsa, 126-7

with yogurt mint sauce, 125

leg,

baked with prunes, 138-9

braised with beans and dates, 120-1

with orzo, 136-7

Lamb (continued):

leg (continued),

stew with garlic and tomatoes, 132-3

stew with green peas and dill, 134-5

Tunisian couscous, 166-7

stew with pearl onions, 140-1

Lasagna, mushroom-spinach goat cheese, 158-9

Leeks:

about, 18

with feta cheese, 36-7

Istanbul, 54

Legumes, about, 17

Lemon, about, 15

Lentils:

about, 17

pilaf with fried zucchini, 162-3

with saffron-scented meat, 118-19

with spicy sausage, 34

Lettuce:

and avocado salad, 50

salad with shallots, 51

Lobster salad, 68

M

Marinated salmon with onion and crème fraîche, 64-5

Mayonnaise, 60

Meat:

about, 17

Meat (continued):

-stuffed green peppers with
  yogurt-cayenne sauce, 130-1

Mint feta phyllo nests, 41

Moroccan-style:

  chicken pie, 108-9

  grapefruit and olive salad, 59

Moussaka, 144-5

Mozzarella cheese:

  broccoli gratin, 28

  bruschetta, 38-9

  mushroom-spinach lasagna,
    158-9

  phyllo nests, 41

Mushrooms:

  and eggplant with penne, 150-1

  garlic shrimp stir-fry, 87

  and green beans stir-fry, 23

  spinach lasagna with goat
    cheese, 158-9

Mussels, paella, 168-70

N

New World chicken cacciatore,
  100-1

Nuts, about, 19

O

Olive oil, about, 14-15

Olives, about, 16

Orzo, lamb stew with, 136-7

Oyster mushrooms, fricassee, 29

P

Paella Rodriguez, 168-70

Pasta:

  with coriander pesto and
    peppers, 152-3

  with spinach and anchovies,
    149

Peaches:

  baked with an almond crust,
    173

  with scallops, 45

Pearl onions, with stewing lamb,
  140-1

Pears, poached, 174

Pellegrino pears, 174

Penne, with eggplant and
  mushrooms, 150-1

Peppercorns, about, 76

Pesto, coriander, 84-5

Phyllo:

  baklava, 180-1

  goat cheese nests, 40

  mint feta nests, 41

  Moroccan chicken pie, 108-9

Pie, chicken, 108-9

Pilaf:

  with apricots and walnuts, 161

  rice and red lentil with fried
    zucchini, 162-3

Pine nuts, about, 19

Poached pears, 174

Polenta, three-cheese, 156-7

Pork:
    chops, hazelnut, 114-15
    ground,
        green peppers stuffed with, 130-1
        with lentils, 118-19
        meat and rice loaf, 142-3
    tenderloin, cassoulet, 122-4
Portobello mushrooms:
    about, 30
    fricassee, 29
    with goat cheese, 30-1
    lasagna with goat cheese, 158-9
Potatoes:
    cauliflower salad, 56-7
    and chickpea stew with spicy sausage, 116-17
    lamb stew with, 134-5
    and tuna salad, 58
Prunes, with baked lamb, 138-9
Pudding, rosewater, 176
Pulses, about, 17

R

Rapini, with paprika, 22
Red lentils:
    about, 17
    pilaf with fried zucchini, 162-3
Red peppers. *See* Bell peppers
Red snapper:
    Barcelona, 80-1
    flash-fried, 82

Rice:
    and black bean stuffed peppers, 164-5
    paella, 168-70
    pilaf with apricots and walnuts, 161
    and red lentil pilaf with fried zucchini, 162-3
Ricotta cheese, three-cheese polenta, 156-7
Romano beans, cassoulet with pork, 122-4
Rosewater pudding, 176

S

Saffron scallops with peach butter, 45
Salads:
    artichoke, 55
    arugula-bocconcini, 52
    bell peppers and seafood, 66-7
    braised green beans and fennel, 24
    cauliflower, 56-7
    chicken, 60-1
    eggplant, 26-7
    grapefruit and black olive, 59
    lettuce and avocado, 50
    lobster, 68
    potato and tuna, 58
    with shallots, 51
    smoked salmon and avocado, 63

Salads (continued):

squid, 62

white kidney beans and tomato, 53

yogurt, 32-3

Salmon:

broiled with green tapenade and endive, 74-5

fish soup, 70-1

with green peppercorn sauce, 76-7

with onion and crème fraîche, 64-5

spaghetti with watercress and, 160

Salsa, garlic keftas with, 126-7

Sardines:

about, 48

with red onion sauce, 48

Sauces:

yogurt, 113

yogurt-cayenne, 130-1

Sautéed eggplant salad, 26-7

Sautéed scallops in wine-lemon sauce, 94

Savory lamb stew with garlic and tomatoes, 132-3

Scallops:

and asparagus gratin, 42-3

and bell pepper salad, 66-7

on eggplant purée, 92-3

with peach butter, 45

in wine-lemon sauce, 94

Seafood, and bell pepper salad, 66-7

See also specific seafood

Shallots, salad with, 51

Shiitake mushrooms, fricassee, 29

Shrimps:

and bell pepper salad, 66-7

fish soup, 70-1

paella, 168-70

Spanish-style, 83

stir-fry with garlic, 87

with tomato and feta, 86

Smoked salmon and avocado salad, 63

Sole, with coriander pesto, 84-5

Soup, fish, 70-1

Spaghetti, with watercress and salmon, 160

Spanish shrimp with paprika, 83

Spices, about, 19

Spicy meat and rice loaf, 142-3

Spicy sausage:

with lentils, 34

Palaio Faliro, 35

potato and chickpea stew, 116-17

Spinach:

and anchovies with pasta, 149

lasagna with goat cheese, 158-9

Squid:

paella, 168-70

salad, 62

See also Calamari

Stew:
  beef with chorizo and
    chickpeas, 128-9
  lamb,
    with green peas and dill,
      134-5
    with pearl onions, 140-1
    with tomatoes, 132-3
  potato and chickpeas with
    sausage, 116-17
Stiffado, 140-1
Stir-fry:
  garlic shrimp, 87
  green bean and mushroom, 23
Strawberries, glazed, 172
Summer artichoke salad, 55
Sun-dried tomatoes:
  about, 16
  green bean and mushroom
    stir-fry, 23
Swordfish:
  with balsamic vinegar, 78
  kebabs with parsley sauce, 79

T

Tagine:
  about, 104
  chicken with lemon, olives and
    grapes, 104-5
Tapenade, 38-9
Three-cheese polenta, 156-7
Tomato paste, about, 16

Tomatoes:
  about, 16
  and braised endive gratinée, 25
  lamb stew with, 132-3
  meat and rice loaf, 142-3
  shrimp and feta, 86
  and white kidney bean salad,
    53
  See also Cherry tomatoes;
    Sun-dried tomatoes
Tuna, and potato salad, 58
Tunisian couscous, 166-7
Turbot, with peppers and olives,
  72

V

Vegetables:
  about, 18-19
  chicken roasted with, 96-7
  Tunisian couscous, 166-7

W

Walnuts:
  about, 19
  -chocolate baklava, 180-1
  raisin cake, 177
Warm salad with shallots, 51
Watercress, spaghetti with
  salmon, 160
White kidney beans:
  braised lamb with, 120-1
  cassoulet with pork, 122-4

White kidney beans (continued):

and tomato salad, 53

Wild mushroom fricassee with rosemary, 29

Wine-simmered chicken with| fennel, 98-9

Y

Yogurt:

-cayenne sauce, 130-1

lamb chops with yogurt sauce, 113

mint sauce, 113, 125

salad, 32-3

Z

Zucchini:

cassoulet with pork and, 122-4

croquettes with yogurt salad, 32-3

with rice and red lentil pilaf, 162-3